THE APOSTLE PAUL

THE APOSTLE PAUL

BY

ALEXANDER WHYTE, D.D.

BAKER BOOK HOUSE
Grand Rapids, Michigan

Reprinted 1977 by
Baker Book House
from the edition issued
by Jennings and Graham

ISBN: 0-8010-9601-4

PHOTOLITHOPRINTED BY CUSHING - MALLOY, INC.
ANN ARBOR, MICHIGAN, UNITED STATES OF AMERICA
1977

TO THE STUDENTS OF DIVINITY

PREFATORY NOTE

As the following sixteen papers form a little study by themselves, it has been thought advisable to separate them from the volume of BIBLE CHARACTERS in which they originally appeared. The rest of the matter belongs to the same line of study.

A. W.

CONTENTS

LECTURES

THE APOSTLE PAUL

SERMONS

WALTER MARSHALL

SIXTEEN LECTURES

THE APOSTLE PAUL

I

PAUL AS A STUDENT

PAUL was not born in the Holy Land like Jesus Christ, and like Peter and James and John. But Paul was proud of his birthplace, as he might very well be. For Tarsus was a great city in a day of great cities. Athens was a great city, Corinth was a great city, and Ephesus was a great city. But Tarsus in some respects was a greater city than any of them. Jerusalem stood alone, and Rome stood alone; but Tarsus engraved herself on her coins as the Metropolis of the East, and her proud claim was not disputed. An immense industry was carried on in the workshops of Tarsus, and an immense import and export trade was carried on in her docks. Nor were the eminent men of Tarsus mere manufacturers and merchants; they were men of education and refinement of manners also. But Saul's father was not one of the eminent men of Tarsus. He was one of the Hebrew dispersion, and he was making his living by the sweat of his brow in that industrious Greek city. And thus it was that Saul his son was far better acquainted with the workshops of Tarsus than with its schools or its colleges. Saul of Tarsus was not born with the silver spoon in his mouth any more than was Jesus of Nazareth, his future Master. It was one of the remarkable laws of that remarkable people that every father was expected, was compelled indeed, to send his son first to a school and then to a workshop. Rich and poor sat on the same school-seat; and rich and poor alike went from school to learn an honest trade. Rabbi Joseph turned the mill. Rabbi Juda was a baker. Rabbi Ada and Rabbi Jose were fishermen ; and, may we not add, Rabbi Peter and Rabbi John ? And so on : woodcutters, leatherdressers, blacksmiths, carpenters. And thus it was that Paul, again and again, held up his hands in the pulpit, and at the prisoner's bar, and said, ' These hands, as you see, are full of callosities and scars, because they have all along ministered to mine own necessities, and to the necessities of those who have been depen- dent on me.'

Saul of Tarsus, like Timothy of Lystra, from a child knew the Holy Scriptures. And thus, no doubt, there was found among his old parchments after his death a Table of Rules and Regulations for his college conduct in Jerusalem, as good as William Law's Rules for his college conduct in Cambridge ; better Rules they could not be. But there is one possibility in Saul's student days in Jerusalem that makes our hearts beat fast in our bosoms to think of it. ' And the Child grew,' we read in a contemporary biography, ' and waxed strong in spirit, filled with wisdom; and the grace of God was upon Him. Now His parents went up to Jerusalem every year at the feast of the passover. And when He was twelve years old, they went up to Jerusalem after the custom of the feast. And it came to pass after three days they found Him in the temple, sitting in the midst of the doctors, both hearing them and asking them questions.' Now Gamaliel would be almost sure to be one of those astonished doctors; and what more likely than that he had taken his best scholar up to the temple to explain the passover to him that day? And did not the young carpenter from Nazareth, and the young weaver from Tarsus, exchange glances of sympathy and shake hands of love that day at the gate of the temple? Are there sports of providence like that in the Divine Mind? asked one of his like-minded students at Rabbi Duncan one day. Yes, and No, was the wise old doctor's answer.

Now the first instruction, as I think, intended to us out of Saul's student days is this—that the finest minds in every generation should study for the Christian ministry. Perhaps the very finest mind that had been born among men since the beginning of the world entered on the study of Old Testament theology when Saul of Tarsus sat down at Gamaliel's feet. And all Saul's fine and fast maturing mind will soon be needed now. For a work lay before that weaver boy of Tarsus second only to the work that lay before that carpenter boy of Nazareth, though second to that by an infinite interval. At the same time, there has been no other work predestinated to mere mortal man to do for God and man to be spoken of in the same day with this weaver boy's fore-ordained work. For even after the Lamb of God had said of His work,—it is finished! how unfinished and incomplete our New Testament would have been without the life and the work of the Apostle Paul. There was a deep harmony pre-established from all eternity between the work of Jesus Christ, and the mind and the heart of Paul His apostle. No other subject in all the world but the Divine Person and the redeeming work of Jesus Christ could have afforded an outlet and an opportunity and an adequate scope for Paul's magnificent mind. While, on the other hand, the law of God and the cross of Christ would have remained to this day but half-revealed mysteries, had it not been for God's revelation of His Son in Paul; and had it not been for Paul's intellectual and spiritual capacity to receive that revelation, and to expound it and preach it. Every man who has read Paul's Epistles with the eyes of his understanding in light, and with his heart on fire, must have continually exclaimed, What a gift to a man is a fine mind, and that mind wholly given up to Jesus Christ! Let our finest minds, then, devote themselves to the study of Christology. Other subjects may, or may not, be exhausted; other callings may, or may not, be overcrowded; but there is plenty of room in the topmost calling of all, and there is an ever-opening and an ever-deepening interest there. No wonder, then, that it has been a University tradition in Scotland that our finest minds have all along entered the Divinity Hall. The other walks and callings of human life both need, and will reward, the best minds that can be spared to them, but let the service of our Lord and Saviour Jesus Christ first be filled. To annotate the Iliad, or the Symposium, or the Commedia; to build up and administer an empire; to command in a battle for freedom by sea or by land; to create and bequeath a great and enriching business; to conduct an influential newspaper; to be the rector of a great school, and so on,—these are all great services done to our generation when we have the talent, and the character, and the opportunity, to do them. But to master Paul, as Paul mastered Moses and Christ; to annotate, and illustrate, and bring freshly home to ten thousand readers, the Galatians, or the Romans, or the Colossians; to have eyes to see what Israel ought to do, and to have the patience, and the courage, to lead a great church to do it; to feed, and to feed better and better for a lifetime, the mind and the heart of a congregation of God's people, and then to depart to be with Christ,—let the finest minds and the deepest and richest hearts in every new generation fall down while they are yet young and say, Lord Jesus, what wilt Thou have me to do with my life, and with whatsoever talents Thou hast intrusted to me?

And, then, the best of all callings being

chosen, the better his mind and the better his heart are, the more profit, to employ Paul's own word about himself, will be made by the true student. For one thing, the better his mind, the more industrious, as a rule, the student of divinity will be. And the absolutely utmost industry in this supreme department of study is simply imperative and indispensable. An unindustrious divinity student should be drummed out of the Hall as soon as he is discovered intruding himself into it. With what a hunger for his books, and with what heavenward vows and oaths of work, young Saul would set out from Tarsus to Jerusalem! Our own best students come up to our divinity seats with thrilling and thanksgiving hearts, and it is only they who have such hearts who can at all enter into Saul's mind and heart and imagination as he descended Olivet and entered Jerusalem and saw his name set down at last on Gamaliel's roll of the sons of the prophets. Gamaliel would have no trouble with Saul, unless it was to supply him with books, and to answer his questions. 'In all my experience I never had a scholar like Saul of Tarsus,' Gamaliel would often afterwards say. And Saul's class-fellows would tell all their days what a help and what a protection it was to be beside Saul. 'We entered the regent's class that year,' writes James Melville in his delightful Diary, 'and he took up Aristotle's *Logic* with us. He had a little boy that served him in his chambers, called David Elistone, who, among thirty-six scholars, so many were we in the class,

was by far the best. This boy he caused to wait
on me and confer with me, and well it was for me,
for his genius and his judgment passed mine as far
as the eagle the owlet. In the multiplication of
propositions, in the conversion of syllogisms, in
the *pons asinorum*, etc., he was as well read as I
was in counting my fingers. This, I mark as a
special cause of thankfulness.' And young Saul of
Tarsus would be just another David Elistone in
Gamaliel's school. And you Edinburgh students
of divinity must be as industrious and as successful
as ever Saul was in Jerusalem, or little Elistone in
St. Andrews. And you have far more reason.
For you have far better teachers, and a far better
subject, and a far better prospect, than ever Saul
had. You are not eternally fore-ordained, indeed,
to write the Epistle to the Romans, or the Epistle
to the Ephesians. But you are chosen, and called,
and matriculated, to do the next best thing to
that. You are called to master those masterpieces
of Paul, so as to live experimentally upon them
all your student life, and then you are to teach
and preach them to your people better and better
all your pulpit and pastoral life. You are to
work with your hands, if need be; you are to sell
your bed, if need be, as Coleridge commands you,
in order to buy Calvin on the Romans, and Luther
on the Galatians, and Goodwin on the Ephesians,
and Davenant on the Colossians, and Hooker on
Justification, and 'that last word on the subject,'
Marshall's *Gospel Mystery of Sanctification*; and
you are to husband-up your priceless and irrecover-

able hours to such studies, as you shall give account at the day of a divinity student's judgment. You are to feed your people, when you have got them committed of Christ to your charge, with the finest of the wheat, and with honey out of the rock. And that, better and better all your life, till your proud people shall make their boast in God about you, as the proud people of Anwoth made their boast about that great genius, and great scholar, and great theologian, and great preacher, and great pastor, Master Samuel Rutherford.

'Give attendance to reading,' was Paul's old-age reminiscence of his student days, in the form of a counsel to young Timothy. 'Paul has not lost his delight in books, even when he is near his death,' says Calvin. And I myself owe so much to good books that I cannot stop myself on this subject as long as I see a single student sitting before me. I have a thousand times had Thomas Boston's experience of good books. 'I plied my books. After earnestly plying my books, I felt my heart begin to grow better. I always find that my health and my heart are the better according as I ply my books.' But you will correct me that Paul could not ply the great books that Thomas Boston plied to his own salvation, and to the salvation of his people in Simprin and Ettrick. Well, then, all the more, ply your pure Bible as Paul and Timothy did, and your profiting, like Paul's profiting and Timothy's, will soon appear unto all. Plying your English Bible even, your profiting will soon appear in your English style, both spoken and written. It will appear in the scriptural stateliness and the holy order of your pulpit prayers also. Your profiting will appear also in the strength, and the depth, and the spirituality, and the experimentalness, and the perennial freshness, of your teaching and your preaching. 'Paul knew his Old Testament so well,' says Dean Farrar in his splendid *Life of St. Paul*, 'that his sentences are constantly moulded by its rhythm, and his thoughts are incessantly coloured by its expressions.'

But, all the time—and it startles and staggers us to hear it—Saul was living in ignorance and in unbelief. They are his own remorseful words, written by his own pen long afterwards—ignorance and unbelief. The finest of minds, the best of educations, sleepless industry, blameless life, and all: with all that, the aged apostle shudders to look back on his student-days of ignorance and unbelief. What in the world does he mean? Strange to say, and it is something for us all to think well about, he declares to us on every auto-biographic page of his, that all the time he sat at Gamaliel's feet, and for many disastrous years after that, he was in the most absolute and woe-working ignorance of the law of God. But that only increases our utter amazement. For, was it not the law of God that Gamaliel had opened his school to teach? What in the world, I ask again, can Paul mean? Have you any idea what the apostle means when he says, with such life-long shame, and such life-long remorse, that all his

Jerusalem and Gamaliel days he was blind and dead in his ignorance of the law of God? It may, perhaps, help us to an understanding of what he means, if we try to mount up and to stand beside him on the far-shining heights of his exalted apostleship, and then look back from thence on his student and Pharisee days in Jerusalem. For it was just in the law of God that Paul afterwards became such a master. It was just the complete abolition of his ignorance of the law of God that set him so high above even the pillar-apostles in their remaining ignorance of it. It was just the law of God that he so reasoned out, and debated with them, as well as taught and preached it with such matchless success in every synagogue from Damascus to Rome. It was his incomparable handling of the law of God that first discovered to himself, and to the enraptured Church of Christ, the apostle's unique theological and philosophical genius, and the whole originality, and depth, and sweep, and grasp, of his matchless mind. An absolutely new world of things was opened up to the Apostolic Church when Paul came back from Arabia with the full revelation of the law and the gospel in his mind, and in his heart, and in his imagination. It was of Paul, and of the law of God in Paul's preaching, that our Lord spake when He said, 'I have yet many things to say unto you, but ye cannot bear them now. Howbeit when He, the Spirit of truth, is come, He will guide you into all truth,'—which He did when He led Paul into

Arabia. And then, after those three reading, meditating, praying, law-discovering, self-discovering, Christ-discovering, years, Paul came back to Damascus, carrying in his mind and in his heart the copestone of New Testament doctrine, with shoutings of grace! grace! unto it. It was Paul's imperial mind, winged as it was with his wonderful imagination, that first swept, full of eyes, over the whole Old Testament history, and saw, down to the bottom and up to the top, the whole hidden mystery of the Old Testament economies, from the creation of the first Adam on to the sitting down of the second Adam at the right hand of God. From the creation of Adam to the call of Abraham; and from the call of Abraham to the giving of the law four hundred and thirty years after; and from the giving of the law till the law was magnified in the life and death of Paul's Master. 'I first of all mortal men have thought the Creator's thoughts after Him,' exclaimed the great astronomical discoverer as he fell on his knees in his observatory. And the great discoverer of the whole mystery of God, in the law and in the gospel, must often have fallen down and uttered the very same exclamation. And his great revelations, and discoveries, and attainments, and experiences, are preserved to us in such profound, axiomatic, and far-enlightening New Testament propositions and illustrations and autobiographic ejaculations as these,—'The law entered that the offence might abound. By the law is the knowledge of sin. The law worketh wrath. Without the law sin was dead. I was alive without the law once. I am sold under sin. The law is our schoolmaster to lead us to Christ. By the works of the law shall no flesh be justified. But now we are no more under the law, but under grace. I am dead to the law, that being dead wherein I was held,'—and so on, through the whole of the Galatians and the Romans, and indeed throughout every Epistle of his. Yes, gentlemen, you may to-night be in as absolute ignorance of all that as the apostle once was; but, I tell you, there still lies scope and opportunity in all that for your most scholarly, most logical, and most philosophical minds, and for your most eloquent, impressive, and prevailing preaching. Till you ascend for yourselves, and then lead your people up to this golden climax of the apostle concerning the law, and concerning Christ, and concerning himself in Christ—this golden climax—'For I through the law am dead to the law, that I might live unto God. I am crucified with Christ: nevertheless I live; yet not I, but Christ liveth in me: and the life I now live in the flesh I live by the faith of the Son of God, who loved me, and gave Himself for me.'

II

PAUL AS APPREHENDED OF CHRIST JESUS

THE first time we see Saul of Tarsus he is silently consenting to Stephen's death. Why the fierce young Pharisee did not take a far more active part in the martyrdom of Stephen we do not know; we can only guess. That a young zealot of Saul's temperament should be content to sit still that day, and merely keep the clothes of the witnesses who stoned Stephen, makes us wonder what it meant. But, beginning with his silent consent to the death of Stephen, Saul soon went on to plan and to perpetrate the most dreadful deeds on his own account. 'As for Saul, he made havoc of the Church, entering into every house, and haling men and women, committed them to prison. Which thing I also did in Jerusalem; and many of the saints did I shut up in prison, and punished them oft in every synagogue, and compelled them to blaspheme. Beyond measure I persecuted the Church of God, and wasted it; I was a blasphemer, and a persecutor, and injurious.' And thus it was that Saul actually went to the high priest in Jerusalem, and desired of him letters to Damascus, to the synagogues, that if he found any of this way, whether they were men or women, he might bring them bound to Jerusalem. And, accordingly, on that errand, out at the Damascus-gate of Jerusalem he rode with his band of temple police behind him: out past Gethsemane: out past Calvary, where he shook his spear in the face of the Crucified, and cried, Aha, aha! Thou deceiver! and posted on breathing out threatenings and slaughter against the disciples of the Lord.

Gird Thy sword upon Thy thigh, O Most Mighty, with Thy glory and Thy majesty! Thine arrows are sharp in the hearts of the King's enemies, whereby the people fall under Thee!

And thus it was that, as Saul journeyed, and came near Damascus, suddenly there shone down upon him a great light from heaven. And he fell to the earth, and heard a voice saying to him, Saul, Saul, why persecutest thou Me? His eyes were as a flame of fire, and His voice as the sound of many waters. And out of His mouth went a sharp two-edged sword, and His countenance was as the sun shineth in his strength. Arise, go into the city, and it shall be told thee what thou shalt do. And Saul arose from the earth, and they led him by the hand, and brought him into Damascus. And he was three days without sight, and did neither eat nor drink. And Ananias entered the house where Saul lay, and putting his hands on him, he said, Brother Saul, the Lord, even Jesus, that appeared unto thee on the way as thou camest, hath sent me, that thou mightest receive thy sight, and be filled with the Holy Ghost. And immediately there fell from his eyes, as if it had been scales, and he received sight forthwith, and arose, and was baptized. Saul of Tarsus, I baptize thee in the name of the Father, and of the Son, and of the Holy Ghost. And there was great joy in the presence of the angels of God over the conversion and the baptism of Saul of Tarsus.

Now, the suddenness of Saul's conversion is the first thing arresting about it to us. It was literally, and in his own words, an 'apprehension.' 'Suddenly,' is his own word about it, as often as he tells us again and again the ever-fresh story of his conversion. The whole subject of conversion is a great study to those who are personally interested in the supremest of all human experiences. There is such a Divine Hand in every conversion; there is such a Sovereignty in it; taking place within a man, there is at the same time such a mysteriousness about it; and, withal, such a transcendent importance, that there is nothing else that ever takes place on the face of the earth for one moment to be compared with a conversion. And, then, there are so many kinds of conversion. So many ways of it, and such different occasions and circumstances of it. Some conversions are as sudden, and as unexpected, and as complete, as Saul's conversion was; and some are slowness itself. Some are such that the very moment, and the very spot, can ever afterwards be pointed out; while some other men are all their days subject to doubt, just because the change came so easy to them as to be without observation. They were born of the Spirit before they could distinguish good from evil, or could discern between their right hand and their left hand. A good sermon will be the occasion of one conversion, a good book of another, and a wise word spoken in due season of another. Hearing a hymn sung, as was the case one Sabbath evening in this very house; hearing a verse read, as was the case with St. Augustine. Just looking for a little at a dry tree will do it sometimes, as was the case with Brother Laurence. Hopeful saw Faithful burned to ashes; Christiana remembered all her surly carriages to her husband; and Mercy came just in time to see Christiana packing up. Their conversions came to Dr. Donne and to Dr. Chalmers long after they were ministers; and, after their almost too late conversion, those two great men became the greatest preachers of their day. A man of business will be on his way to his office on a Monday morning, and he could let you see to this day the very shop window, passing which, in Princes Street, he was apprehended. I was engaged to be married and she died, said a young communicant to me on one occasion. It was the unkindness of my mistress, said a servant-girl. Just as I am writing these lines this letter reaches me: 'When the Lord opened my eyes the sight I saw broke me down completely. I tried to work myself right, till it turned out to be the hardest task I ever tried. But I would not give in till He took me by the coat-neck and held me over hell. Oh, sir, it was a terrible time! My sense of sin drove me half mad. But I kept pouring out my heart in prayer!' And then my correspondent goes on to tell me the name of the book that was made such a blessing to him. And then he asks that his mistakes in spelling be pardoned, and signs himself an office-bearer in the Church of one of my friends. But you will go over for yourselves all the cases of conversion you have ever heard about, or read about, and you will see for yourselves how full of all kinds of individuality, and variety, and intensity of interest, the work of conversion is, till like Mercy in *The Pilgrim's Progress*, you will fall in love with your own.

Some men put off their conversion because they have no sense of sin. But look at Saul. What sense of sin had he? Not one atom. He was an old and a heaven-ripe apostle before his full sense of sin came home to him. He was not groaning out the seventh of the Romans when he was galloping at the top of his speed on his way to Damascus. A sensibility to sin so exquisite and so spiritual as that of the apostle never yet came to any man but after long long years of the holiest of lives. To ninety-nine out of a hundred, even of truly converted men, it never comes at all. How could it? At the same time, who knows? your conversion, both in its present insensibility, and in its subsequent spirituality, may be to be of the same kind as Paul's was, if you will only on the spot submit to it. Accept your offered conversion, and go home and act at once and ever after upon it, and trust the Holy Ghost for your sense of sin. And if you belong to the same mental and moral and spiritual seed of Israel as Paul, your sense of sin will yet come to you with a vengeance. And, once it begins to come, it will never cease coming more and more, till you will almost be driven beside yourself with it. On the other hand, your conversion may not be to be of the heart-breaking kind. You may not be to be held over open hell by the coat-neck like my ill-spelling friend; your experience may be to be like that of Lydia. Like hers, your conversion may be to steal in upon your heart some night at a prayer-meeting,—be it of whatever kind it is to be, take it when and where it is offered to you. And if your conversion is of the right kind at all, and holds, you will in due time and in your due order, get your fit and proper share of that saving grace, of which you say you are so utterly empty to-night.

But not only had Saul no sense of sin to prepare him for his conversion: he had no preparation and no fitness for his conversion, of any kind whatsoever. He brought nothing in his hands. He came just as he was. He was without one plea. Poor, wretched, blind; sight, riches, healing of the mind. Read his thrice-told story, and see if there is any lesson plainer, or more pointed to you in it all, than just the unexpectedness, the unpreparedness, and the completeness on the spot, of Saul's conversion. With, on the other hand, his instantaneous and full faith, his childlike trust, his full assurance, and his prompt and unquestioning obedience. Yes, it is just the absolute sovereignty, startling suddenness, total unpreparedness, entire undeservingness, and glorious completeness, of Saul's conversion that, all taken together, make it such a study, and, in some respects, such a model conversion, to you and to me.

There is another lesson told us three times, as if to make sure that we shall not miss it nor mistake it. Saul got his conversion out of that overthrow on the way to Damascus, while all his companions only got some bodily bruises from their fall, and the complete upsetting of their errand, out of it. The temple officers had each his own story to tell when they returned without any prisoners to Jerusalem : only, none of them needed to be led by the hand into Damascus, and none of them were baptized by Ananias, but Saul only. All of which is written for our learning. For the very same thing will take place here to-night. One will be Saul over again, and those who are sitting beside him will be Saul's companions over again. One will go straight home after this service, and will never all his days have Saul's sudden and unexpected conversion out of his mind, such a divine pattern is it to be to him of his own conversion. While his companions will be able to tell when they go home who preached, and on what, the fulness of the Church, the excellence of the music, and the state of the weather on the way home—and that will be all. 'And they that were with me saw indeed the light, and were afraid; but they heard not the voice of Him that spake with me. And I said, What shall I do, Lord? And He said to me, Arise, and go into the city, and there it shall be told thee of all things which are appointed for thee to do.'

'It is a trap set for us,' said Ananias. 'Lord,' he said, 'I have heard by many of this man, how much evil he hath done to Thy saints in Jerusalem. And how he has come here with authority to bind all that call upon Thy name. It is a trap set for our destruction,' said Ananias. 'Go to the street called Straight,' said the Lord, 'and if thou dost not find him in prayer, then it is a trap as thou fearest it is.' The mark of Saul's conversion that silenced Ananias was this, that Saul had been three days and three nights in fasting and in prayer without ceasing. Behold he prayeth, said Christ, proud of the completeness and the success of His conversion of Saul. Has Jesus Christ, with His eyes like a flame of fire, set that secret mark on your conversion and on mine? Does he point you out to His ministering angels and sympathising saints in heaven to-night, as He pointed out Saul to Ananias? How does your conversion stand the test of secret prayer? Behold, he prayeth! said

Christ. And unceasing prayer, both for himself and for all his converts, remained to be Paul's mark, and token, and seal, down to the end of his days.

The best expositor by far that ever took Paul's epistles up into a pulpit, has said that the apostle never fell into a single inconsistency after his conversion. Now, with all submission, I cannot receive that even about Paul, any more than I can receive it about any other man that ever was converted on the face of this earth. That He never fell into a single inconsistency could only be said about One Man; and we never speak about His conversion. But the very fact that the profoundest preacher that I possess on Paul, and the profoundest preacher of conversion-consistency, has said such a thing as that, shows us what a splendid, what a complete, and what a consistent, conversion Paul's conversion must have been. How thoroughgoing it must have been at the time; and how holy in all manner of walk and conversation must Paul have lived ever after. Speaking here for myself, and not venturing to speak for any of you, when I read a thing like that, and a thing said by such a master in Israel as he was who said that, and then look at my own life in the searching light of that, I feel as if I can never up till now have been converted myself at all. Unless this also is a sure mark of a true conversion, which I have seen set down with incomparable power by this very same master in Israel, this,—that it is a sure and certain mark of a true conversion that no man ever

33

understands what inconsistency really is till he is truly converted. To be all but entirely void of offence, as Paul said of himself; to be all but completely consistent in everything, was one of the sure and certain marks of Paul's conversion. But, then, to feel myself to be full to the lips of offence : to see and to feel myself to be the most inconsistent man in all the world, is, by this same high authority, offered to me as a mark of my conversion, as good to me as Paul's magnificent marks were to him. 'The disproportion of man' is one of Pascal's most prostrating passages; and the offensiveness, the inconsistency, and the disproportion, of my heart and my life, are the most prostrating of all my experiences. Indeed, nothing ever prostrates me, to be called prostration, but these experiences. At the same time, the whole and entire truth at its deepest bottom is this. That both things are true of Paul and of his conversion. Paul was at one and the same moment, and in one and the same matter, both the most consistent, and the most inconsistent, of all Christ's converts. He was both the most blameless, and the most blameable; the best proportioned, and the most disproportioned, of all Christian men, such was the holiness of his life, and such was the spirituality of his mind and heart. And both experiences, taken together, combine to constitute the most complete and all-round mark of a perfect conversion. Now, all that, and far more than all that, combine to make Paul's conversion the most momentous, and the most wonderful, conversion in all the world.　And yet, no.　There is one other conversion long since Paul's, that will, to you and to me to all eternity, quite eclipse Paul's conversion, and will for ever completely cast, even it, quite into the shade.

III

PAUL IN ARABIA

NO sooner was Paul baptized by Ananias, than, instead of returning home to Jerusalem, he immediately set out for Arabia. He had come down to Damascus with horses and servants like a prince, but he set out alone for Arabia like Jacob with his staff. For, all that he took with him was his parchments, and some purchases he had made in the street called Straight. A few of those simple instruments that tentmakers use when they have to minister to their own necessities, was all that Paul encumbered himself with as he started from Ananias's door on his long and solitary journey to Arabia.

What it was that took Paul so immediately and so far away as Arabia, we can only guess. If it was simply a complete seclusion that he was in search of, he might surely have secured that seclusion much nearer home. But, somehow, Sinai seems to have drawn Paul to her awful solitudes with an irresistible attraction and strength. It may have been an old desire of his formed at Gamaliel's feet, some day to see the Mount of God with his own eyes. He may have said to himself

37

that he must hide himself for once in that cleft-rock before he sat down to his life-work in Moses' seat. I must see Rome, he said towards the end of his life. I must see Sinai, he also said at the beginning of his life. And thus it was that as soon as he was baptized in Ananias's house in Damascus, Paul immediately set out for Arabia.

Look at that weak bodily presence. But, at the same time, judge him not by his outward appearance. For he carries Augustine, and Luther, and Calvin, and Knox, and Edwards, and Chalmers, in his fruitful loins. In that lonely stranger you are now looking at, and in his seed, shall all the families of the earth be blessed. Look at the eyes of his understanding as they begin to be enlightened. Look at him with his heart all on fire. Look at him as he unrolls his parchments at every roadside well, and drinks of the brook by the way. Thy word is more to me than my necessary food, and thy love is better than wine!

What a three years were those three years that Paul spent in Arabia! Never did any other lord receive his own again with such usury as when Paul went into Arabia with Moses and the Prophets and the Psalms in his knapsack, and returned to Damascus with the Romans and the Ephesians and the Colossians in his mouth and in his heart. What an incomparable book waits to be written about those three immortal years in Arabia! After those thirty preparation-years at Nazareth, there is no other opportunity left for any sanctified pen, like those three revelation-years in Arabia. Only,

it will demand all that is within the most Paul-like
writer, to fit him out for his splendid enterprise.
It will demand, and it will repay, all his learning,
and all his intellect, and all his imagination, and
all his sinfulness, and all his salvation. Just to
give us a single Sabbath out of Paul's hundred and
fifty Sabbaths at Sinai—what a revelation to us that
would be! It would be something like this, only
a thousand times better. When first you fell in
love: when first your captivated heart made you
like the chariots of Ammi-nadib; the whole world
was full of one name to you. There was no other
name to you in all the world. Every bird sang
that name. Every rock echoed with that name.
You wrote that name everywhere. You read that
name everywhere. You loved everybody and everything for the sake of that name. Now, it was
something like that between Paul and Jesus Christ.
Only, it was far better than that between Paul
and Jesus Christ at the time, and it was far more
lasting with them than it has been with you.
Luther, who was almost as great a lover of Jesus
Christ as Paul was, has this over and over again
about Paul and Jesus Christ. 'Jesus Christ is never
out of Paul's mouth. Indeed, there is nobody and
nothing now and always in Paul's mouth but Jesus
Christ and His Cross.' Now that is literally true.
For, as often as Paul opens his Moses in Arabia, and
finds the place he is seeking for, he cannot see the
place when he has found it for Jesus Christ.
Jesus Christ comes between Paul and everything.
To Paul to read, and to meditate, and to pray, is

Jesus Christ. So much so, that as soon as he finds the place at the very first verse of Genesis, he immediately goes off at the word, and exclaims, till the Arabs all around listen to his rapture,—the mystery! he exclaims, which from the beginning of the world hath been hid in God, who created all things by Jesus Christ. And at this,—Let there be light! For God, he exclaims again, who commanded the light to shine out of darkness, hath shined in our hearts in the face of Jesus Christ. And, does Adam burst out into his bridegroom doxology,—This is now bone of my bone, and flesh of my flesh!—then Paul instantly adds, Amen! But I speak concerning Christ and His Church. And before he leaves the first Adam he gets such a revelation of the second Adam made in him that the Corinthians had many a glorious Sabbath morning on the two Adams, all the way from Arabia, long afterwards. And, again, no sooner does God speak in covenant to Abraham about his seed, than Paul immediately annotates that He saith not to seeds as of many, but as of One, which is Christ. But, on all that Moses ever wrote, there was nothing that Paul spent so much time and strength, as just on this concerning the father of the faithful,—that Abraham believed in God, and it was counted to him for righteousness. Now, said Paul, reasoning to himself over that revelation, and then reasoning to us,—Now it was not written for Abraham's sake alone, that it was imputed to him, but for our sakes also, to whom it shall be imputed, if we believe on Him who raised up Jesus our Lord from the dead; who was delivered for our offences, and was raised again for our justification. And so on, till to have spent a single Sabbath-day with Paul at Sinai would have been almost as good as to have walked that evening hour to Emmaus. So did Paul discover the Son of God in Arabia: so did Paul have the Son of God revealed to him in Adam, and in Abraham, and in Moses, and in David, and in Isaiah, but, best of all, in Paul himself.

And, then, Paul's first fast-day in Arabia. Paul was never out of the Psalms on those days that he observed so solemnly at Sinai. Till his David was like John Bunyan's Luther, so old that it was ready to fall piece from piece if he did but turn it over. But he always turned it over at such sacramental seasons till he came again to that great self-examination Psalm, where he found it written concerning himself: These things hast thou done, and I kept silence. Thou thoughtest that I was altogether such an one as thyself. But I will reprove thee, and set them in order before thee. And it was so. For, there they stood, set in order before him, and passed in order before him and before God. The souls of all the men and women and children he had haled to prison, and had compelled to blaspheme, and had slain with the sword. And, then, as he hid himself in the cleft rock—how the Name of the LORD would come up into his mind . and how, like Moses also, he would make haste and bow his head to the earth and say: Take me for one of Thy people. And, till God would again reveal His Son in Paul in a way, and to a degree, that it is not possible for Paul to tell to such impenitent and unprostrated readers of his as we are. And, then, far over and above those terrible sins of his youth, there was the absolutely unparalleled and absolutely indescribable agony that came upon Paul out of the remaining covetousness and consequent malice of his heart, and more and more so as his heart was more and more brought down under the ever-increasing and all-piercing spirituality of God's holy law. An agony that sometimes threatened to drive Paul beside himself altogether. And till, on the rocks of Sinai the shepherds would sometimes come on somewhat the same sweat of blood that the gardeners came on in the Garden of Gethsemane. For it was in Arabia, and it was under the Mount of God, that Paul's apostolic ink-horn was first filled with that ink of God with which he long afterwards wrote that so little understood writing of his, which we call the Seventh of the Romans. A little understood writing ; and no wonder !

The Apostle came back from Arabia to Damascus, after three years' absence, absolutely ladened down with all manner of doctrines, and directions, and examples, for us and for our salvation, if we would only attend to them and receive them. Directions and examples of which this is one of the first. That solitude, the most complete and not short solitude, was the one thing that Paul determined to secure for himself immediately after his conversion and his baptism.

And we have a still better Example of all that
than even Paul. For, over and above His thirty
uninvaded years, no sooner was that 'Glorious
Eremite' baptized, than he went away and took
forty days to Himself before He began His public
life. 'One day'—sings concerning Him one of
His servants who loved seclusion also, and put
it to some purpose—

> ' One day forth walked alone, the Spirit leading,
>   And His deep thoughts, the better to converse
>   With solitude ; till far from track of man,
>   Thought following thought, and step on step led on,
>   He entered now the bordering desert-wild,
>   And, with dark shades and rocks environ'd round,
>   His holy meditations thus pursued.'

And thus it is that Holy Scripture is everywhere so full of apartness and aloneness and
solitude : of lodges in the wilderness, and of
shut doors in the city: of early mornings, and
late nights, and lonely night-watches : of Sab-
bath-days and holidays, and all such asylums of
spiritual retreat.

> Down to Gehenna, and up to the throne,
> He travels the fastest who travels alone.

But the Apostle's chief reason for telling us
about Arabia at all is this, to prove to us, and to
impress upon us, that it was not cities and
colleges and books that made him what by that
time he was made. It was God Himself who
made Paul the Apostle he was made. I conferred not with flesh and blood, he protests.

He had books, indeed, as we have seen : he always had. He had the best of books : he always had. But even Moses and David and Isaiah themselves are but flesh and blood compared with God. Even grace itself is but flesh and blood compared with Christ, says Thomas Shepard. And Paul is careful and exact, above everything, to make it clear to us, that not only was it God Himself who immediately and conclusively revealed His Son in Paul ; but, also, that it was His Son that God so revealed. It was not Jesus Christ, so much, distinguishes Paul, that God revealed in him. Jesus Christ had revealed Himself to Paul already at the gate of Damascus, but God's revelation of His Son in Arabia was a revelation of far more than of Jesus Christ whom Paul was persecuting. For, this in Arabia is God's Eternal and Co-Equal Son. And that, not merely as made flesh, and made sin : not merely as crucified, and risen, and exalted, and glorified ; but as He had been before all that, and during all that, and after all that. It was God's Essential and Eternal Son : it was God's very deepest, completest, and most crowning revelation possible of His only-begotten Son, that God, in such grace and truth, made in Paul in Arabia.

In me, says Paul. In my deepest mind and in my deepest heart : in my very innermost soul and strength. And thus it was that Paul underwent two grand revelations, over and above a multitude of lesser revelations which arose out of those two epoch-making revelations, and which both perfected and applied them. The one, that grand and epoch-making revelation made on the way to Damascus, and made immediately by Jesus Christ, whom Paul was at that moment persecuting. A revelation divinely suited to all the circumstances. A revelation outward, arresting, overpowering: taking possession of all the persecutor's bodily senses, and thus surrounding and seizing all the passes into his soul. The other, made within and upon Paul's pure and naked soul, and apart altogether from the employment of his senses upon his soul. A revelation impossible adequately to describe. A revelation made by God of His Son, most inward, most profound, most penetrating, most soul-possessing: most-enlarging to the soul, most uplifting, and most upholding: most assuring, most satisfying, most sanctifying: intellectual, spiritual, experimental, evangelical: all-renewing and all-transforming: full of truth, full of love, full of assurance, full of holiness, full of the peace of God, which passeth all understanding. Jesus of Nazareth appeared *to* Saul the persecutor, as He had already appeared to Mary Magdalene, and to the ten disciples, and to Thomas. But God the Father revealed His Son *in* Paul the Apostle, as He had never revealed Him before, and as He has never revealed Him since in mortal man. That is to say, with a fulness, and with a finalness, that has made all God's subsequent revelations of His Son, at their best, to be but superficial and partial, occasional and intermittent. Not that it need be so Not that it ought to be so. For if we but gave ourselves up to God and to His Son, as Paul gave himself up, we also, no doubt, would soon reap our reward. But, as it is, Paul's apprehension of God's Son, Paul's comprehension of God's Son, and Paul's service of God's Son, have remained to this day, by far the first, by far the best, by far the most complete, by far the most final, and by far the most fruitful, revelation of His Son, that Almighty God has ever made in any of the sons of men.

IV

PAUL'S VISIT TO JERUSALEM TO SEE PETER

PUT yourself back into Paul's place. Suppose yourself born in Tarsus, brought up at Gamaliel's feet in Jerusalem, and keeping the clothes of Stephen's executioners. Think of yourself as a blasphemer, and a persecutor, and injurious. And then imagine yourself apprehended of Christ Jesus, driven of the Spirit into the wilderness of Arabia, and coming back with all your bones burning within you to preach Jesus Christ and Him crucified. But, all the time, you have never once seen your Master in the flesh, as His twelve disciples had seen Him. He had been for thirty years with His mother and His sisters and His brethren in Galilee. And then He had been for three years with the twelve and the seventy. But Paul had been born out of due time. And thus it was that Paul went up to Jerusalem to see Peter about all that. Paul had a great desire to see Peter about all that before he began his ministry. And you would have had that same great desire, and so would I.

At the same time, even with the prospect of seeing Peter, it must have taken no little courage

47

on Paul's part to face Judea and Jerusalem again.
To face the widows and the orphans of the men he
had put to death in the days of his ignorance and
unbelief. To Paul the very streets of Jerusalem
were still wet with that innocent blood. Led in
by Peter, Paul sat at the same Lord's table, and
ate the same bread, and drank the same wine, with
both old and young communicants, who had not
yet put off their garments of mourning because of
Paul. Deliver me from blood-guiltiness, O God,
Thou God of my salvation. Then will I teach
transgressors Thy ways. Do good in Thy good
pleasure unto Zion; build Thou the walls of
Jerusalem. And thus it was that, to the end of
his days, Paul was always making collections for
those same poor saints that were in Jerusalem.
Paul would have pensioned every one of them out
of his own pocket, had he been able. But how
could he do that off a needle and a pair of shears?
And thus it was that he begged so incessantly for
the fatherless families that he had made fatherless
in Judea and in Jerusalem. Now, if any of you
have ever made any woman a widow, or any child
an orphan, or done anything of that remorseful
kind, do not flee the country. You cannot do it,
and you need not try. Remain where you are.
Go back to the place. Go back often in imagination, if not in your bodily presence. Do the very
utmost that in you lies, to repair the irreparable
wrong that you did long ago. And, when you
cannot redeem that dreadful damage, commit it to
Him who can redeem both it and you. And say

to Him continually:—Count me a partner with Thee. And put that also down to my account.

'To see Peter,' our Authorised Version is made to say. 'To visit Peter,' the Revised Version is made to say. And, still, to help out all that acknowledged lameness, the revised margin is made to say, 'to become acquainted with Peter.' But Paul would not have gone so far, at that time at any rate, to see Peter or any one else. Any one else, but Peter's Master. But to see Him even once, as He was in the flesh, Paul would have gone from Damascus to Jerusalem on his hands and his knees. 'I went up to Jerusalem to *history* Peter,' is what Paul really says. Only, that is not good English. But far better bad English, than an utterly meaningless translation of such a text. 'To interview Peter,' is not good English either, but it conveys Paul's meaning exactly. The great Greek historians employ Paul's very identical word when they tell their readers the pains they took to get first-hand information before they began to write their books. 'I went up to interrogate and to cross-question Peter all about our Lord,' that would be rough English indeed, but it would be far better than so feebly to say, 'to see Peter,' which positively hides from his readers what was Paul's real errand to Jerusalem, and to Peter.

Had Landor been led to turn his fine dramatic genius and his ripe scholarship to Scriptural subjects, he would, to a certainty, have given us the conversations that took place for fifteen days between Paul and Peter. Landor's Epictetus and

Seneca, his Diogenes and Plato, his Melanchthon
and Calvin, his Galileo and Milton and a Domini-
can, and his Dante and Beatrice, are all among his
masterpieces. But his Paul and Peter, and his
Paul and James the brother of our Lord, and
especially his Paul and the mother of our Lord,
would have eclipsed clean out of sight his most
classical compositions. For, on no possible subject,
was Peter so ready always to speak, and to all
comers, as just about his Master. And never
before nor since had Peter such a hungry hearer
as just his present visitor and interrogator from
Arabia and Damascus. Peter began by telling
Paul all about that day when his brother Andrew
so burst in upon him about the Messiah. And
then that day only second to it, on the Lake of
Gennesaret. And then Matthew the publican's
feast, and so on, till Peter soon saw what it was
that Paul had come so far to hear. And then he
went on with the good Samaritan, and the lost
piece of silver, and the lost sheep, and the lost son.
For fifteen days and fifteen nights this went on
till the two prostrate men took their shoes off
their feet when they entered the Garden of Gethsemane. And both at the cock-crowing, and at
Calvary, Peter and Paul wept so sore that Mary
herself, and Mary Magdalene, did not weep like
it. Now, just trust me and tell me what you
would have asked at Peter about his Master.
Would you have asked anything? How far would
you go to-night to have an interview with Peter?
Honestly, have you any curiosity at all about

Jesus Christ, either as He is in heaven now, or as He was on earth then? Really and truly, do you ever think about Him, and imagine Him, and what He is saying and doing? Or are you like John Bunyan, who never thought whether there was a Christ or no? If you would tell me two or three of the questions you would have put to Peter, I would tell you in return just who and what you are; just how you stand to-night to Jesus Christ, and how He stands to you: and what He thinks and says about you, and intends toward you.

And then if Mary, the mother of our Lord, was still in this world, it is certain to me that Paul both saw her in James's house, and kissed her hand, and called her Blessed. You may depend upon it that Mary did not remain very long away from James's house after his conversion. It was all very good to have a lodging with the disciple whom Jesus loved, till her own slow-hearted son believed. But I put it to you who are mothers in Israel, to put yourselves in Mary's place in those days, and to say if you would have been to be found anywhere, by that time, but in the house of your own believing son. And what more sure and certain than that God, here again, revealed His Son to Paul out of Mary's long hidden heart. 'I have the most perfect, and at first-hand, assurance of all these things from them that were eye-witnesses and ministers of the Word,' says Paul's physician and private secretary. No-where, at any rate, in the whole world, could that

51

miraculous and mystery-laden woman have found such another heart as Paul's into which to pour out all that had been for so long sealed up in her hidden heart. 'Whether we were in the body, or out of the body, as she told me all about Nazareth, and as I told her all about Damascus and Arabia, I cannot tell : God knoweth.'

'From the Old Testament point of view,' says Bengel in his own striking and suggestive way, 'the progress is made from the knowledge of Christ to the knowledge of Jesus. From the New Testament point of view, the progress is made from the knowledge of Jesus to the knowledge of Christ.' And have we not ourselves already seen how Paul's progress was made? Paul's progress was made from the knowledge of Jesus of Nazareth risen from the dead, to the knowledge of the Son of God; and then from the knowledge of both back to the knowledge of the Holy Child Jesus, and the Holy Man Jesus, as He was known to His mother, to James His brother, and to Peter His so intimate disciple. Paul went 'back to Jesus,' as the saying sometimes is ; but when he went back he took back with him all the knowledge of the Son of God that he has put into his Epistles, ay, and much more than the readers of his Epistles were able to receive. And God's way with Paul is His best way with us also. You will never read the four Gospels with true intellectual understanding, and with true spiritual appreciation, till you have first read and understood and appreciated Paul's Epistles. But after

you have had God's Son revealed in you by means
of Paul's Epistles, you will then be prepared for
all that Matthew and Mark and Luke and John
have to tell you about the Word made flesh in
their day. Paul's hand holds the true key to all
the mysteries that are hid in the Prophets and in
the Psalms and in the Gospels. Take back Paul
with you, and all the prophecies and all the types
of the Old Testament, and all the wonderful works
of God in the New Testament,—His Son's sinless
conception, His miracles, His teaching and preaching, His agony in the garden, His death on the
Cross, and His resurrection and ascension,—will
all fall into their natural and necessary places.
It is in the very same order in which the great
things of God were revealed to Paul, and apprehended by Paul, that they will best be revealed to
us, and best apprehended by us. First our conversion; and then the Pauline, Patristic, and
Puritan doctrine of the Son of God; and then all
that taken back by us to the earthly life of our
Blessed Lord as it is told to us by the four
Evangelists. Damascus, Arabia, Nazareth, Jerusalem,—this, in our day also, is the God-guided
progress, in which the true successors of the
Apostle Paul are still travelling, in their spiritual
experience, and in their evangelical scholarship.

V

PAUL AS A PREACHER

WHEN it pleased God to reveal the cross of
Christ in Paul, from that day the cross
of Christ was Paul's special, peculiar, and exclusive,
Gospel. The cross of Christ is ' my gospel,' Paul
proudly and constantly claims, in the face of all
comers. The cross of Christ, he declares, is the
one and the only Gospel that he preaches, that he
always preaches, and that he alone preaches. The
cross of Christ was profitable to Paul for doctrine,
for reproof, for correction, and for instruction in
righteousness : and nothing else was of any real
interest or any real profit to Paul. The cross of
Christ was the alpha and the omega, the beginning, and the middle, and the end, of all Paul's
preaching. Paul drew all his doctrines, and all
his instructions, and all his reproofs, out of the
cross of Christ. He drew his profound and
poignant doctrines of the sinfulness of sin, and
the consequent misery of man, out of the cross of
Christ. He saw and he felt all that in himself,
and in the whole world ; but the cross of Christ
gave a new profundity, and a new poignancy, to
all that to him. He drew his incomparably

magnificent doctrines of the grace of God and the love of Christ out of the cross of Christ : those doctrines of his in the preaching of which he bursts out into such rapturous doxologies. The whole of the life of faith also, in all its manifoldness, and in all its universalness, and his own full assurance of everlasting life,—all that, and much more than all that, Paul, by his splendid genius, and it all so splendidly sanctified and inspired, drew out of the cross of Christ. Take away the cross of Christ from Paul, and he is as weak as any other man. Paul has nothing left to preach if you take away from him the cross of Christ. His mouth is shut. His pulpit is in ruins. His arm is broken. He is of all men most miserable. But let God reveal the cross of Christ in Paul, and, straightway, he can both do, and endure, all things. Paul is henceforth debtor both to the Greeks and to the Barbarians ; both to the wise, and to the unwise. Once reveal the cross of Christ in Paul, and you thereby lay a life-long necessity upon him. Yea, woe is unto him, ever after, if he preaches not the Gospel of the cross of Christ.

We preach not ourselves, Paul asserts with a good conscience in another sermon of his. And yet, at the same time, he introduces himself into almost every sermon he preaches. Paul simply cannot preach the cross of Christ as he must preach it, without boldly bringing himself in, as both the best pattern and the best proof of what the cross of Christ can do. Paul's salvation,—the absolute graciousness of Paul's salvation, and his absolute assurance of it,—these things are the infallible marks of their authenticity that Paul prints upon every Epistle of his. The cross of Christ, and Paul's salvation by that cross, are the two constant, and complementary, topics of Paul's pulpit ; they are but the two sides of Paul's shield of salvation. The most beautiful English preacher of the past generation has told us that his conversion was so absorbing and so abiding that it made him rest ever after in the thought of two, and two only absolute and luminously self-evident beings, himself and his Creator. And so it was with Paul's conversion also. Only, in Paul's case it was not so much his Creator who was so luminously self-evident to Paul, it was much more his Redeemer. And thus it was that in Paul's preaching there were always present those two luminously self-evident subjects, Paul's sin and Christ's cross : Paul the chief of sinners, and Jesus Christ and Him crucified. And thus it is that Paul's so profound, and so experimental, preaching so satisfies us. And thus it is also that it alone satisfies us. When we are pining away under some secret disease if our physician comes and mocks at all our misery ; if he treats our mortal wound as all imagination ; if he rebukes and abuses us as if it were all so much melancholy, —our hearts know their own bitterness. But if we fall into the hands of a wise man and a sound and skilful physician, he at once takes in the whole seriousness of our case. Before we have opened our mouth about ourselves, he has already laid his

hand on our hurt, and has said to us,—Thou art
ill to death indeed. Thy whole head is sick and
thy whole heart faint. And already we feel that
there is hope. At any rate, we are not to die
under the hands of a charlatan. And Paul is the
furthest of all our physicians from a charlatan.
Paul rips open all the dark secrets of our consciences, and all the hidden rottennesses of our
hearts, till he is the one preacher of all preachers
for us. And his the Gospel of all Gospels. At
any rate, speaking for myself, as often as my own
sin and misery, impossible to be told, again close
in upon me till my broken heart cries out, Oh,
wretchedest of men that I am! Paul is instantly
at my bedside with the cross of Christ, and with
his own case told to me to fetch back my life to
me. Paul's prescription, as the physicians call it,
never fails me. Never. As often as seventy times
seven, every mortal day of mine, the amazement
and the misery of my sinfulness overwhelms me,
Paul no sooner sets forth to me Jesus Christ and
Him crucified, than a great light falls on my
amazement, and a great alleviation on my misery.
It is a dark light. It is a dreadful light. It is a
light like a drawn sword. But it *is* light, where
no other light from heaven, or from earth, could
give a ray of light to me. At the cross, before
the cross, under the cross, upon the cross, I am reconciled to God, and God is reconciled to me. I
am reconciled to you also, and you to me. All
the hand-writings in heaven and earth and hell,
that were so bitter against me, are all blotted out

by His blood. All my injustices to you and all my injuries from you; all my animosities, antipathies, alienations, retaliations, distastes, and dislikes, all are rooted up out of my heart by the cross of Christ. For I am slain to myself because of the cross of Christ. The one and only cause of all my unspeakable sinfulness and misery,—myself; I, myself, am slain to death for ever by the cross of Christ. My self-love, my self-will, my self-seeking, my self-pleasing, they are all slain; or what is as good, they have got their sure deathblow by the cross of Christ. I am crucified with Christ: nevertheless I live; yet not I, but Christ liveth in me: and the life which I now live in the flesh, I live by the faith of the Son of God, who loved me, and gave Himself for me.

He alone is a 'right divine' who can preach this faith of the Son of God properly, says Luther. He is a 'right preacher' who can distinguish, first to himself, and then to his people, faith from the law, and grace from works, says the Reformer. Now Paul was a right divine and he was the first father and forerunner of all such. And never more so than when he is putting forth all his stupendous power to preach that divinest doctrine of his, that our best obedience, if offered in the very least measure for our salvation, is a complete abandonment, and a fatal denial of the cross of Christ. Some men will start up at that, and will protest at it, and debate against it. So did Paul as long as he was still alive, and kept the clothes of them that stoned Stephen. And so did I for

a long time. But now that greatest and best of
all Paul's doctrines of grace, as often as I come on
it in its bud in Abraham, and in its full flower
and fruit in Paul and in Luther, it makes my
heart to sing and dance within me. And it comes
to me from the God of my salvation a thousand
times every day. Why was that blessed doctrine
so long in being preached by some right divine to
me? Why was I, myself, so long in learning and
in preaching this first principle of the doctrine of
Christ? And why do I go back so often, to this
day, to Moses and to myself? I have a desire to
depart and to be with Christ, says Paul to the
Philippians. And so have I. But, before God,
I lie not. He is my witness, that I beseech Him
every day about this very matter, and about little
besides. I beseech Him every hour of the day,
that I may be spared for some more years yet, in
order that I may grow, as I have never yet grown,
into this selfsame faith of the Son of God. Into
the faith that justifies the ungodly, and sanctifies
the sinful, and brings love, and peace, and joy, and
hope, and full assurance of everlasting life, to my
soul. And to preach all that as I have never yet
preached it : and, then, you would perhaps take
my epitaph out of Luther on the Galatians, and
would write this sentence over me—'Come, and
see, all ye that pass by, for here lies a right
divine.' Why is it that this epitaph is so seldom
to be read in any of our churchyards over our
ministers? Why are there so few divines so right
in Scotland as to satisfy Paul and Luther? Why

are there so few of our young preachers who make Paul's determination, and stand to it? As often as I think of this great determination of his, I always remember Hooker's immortal sermon on Justification. Hooker, in this matter at any rate, was a right Pauline and Lutheran divine. And what does that master in Israel, and that equal master of an English style, say to us on this point? Every preacher of Christ, and of faith in the cross of Christ, should have this passage printed indelibly on his heart. 'CHRIST HATH MERITED RIGHTEOUSNESS FOR AS MANY AS ARE FOUND IN HIM. AND IN HIM GOD FINDETH US, IF WE BE FAITHFUL; FOR BY FAITH WE ARE INCORPORATED INTO HIM. THEN, ALTHOUGH WE BE IN OURSELVES ALTOGETHER SINFUL AND UNRIGHTEOUS, YET EVEN THE MAN WHO IS IN HIMSELF IMPIOUS, FULL OF INIQUITY, FULL OF SIN; HIM BEING FOUND IN CHRIST THROUGH FAITH, AND HAVING HIS SIN IN HATRED THROUGH REPENTANCE, HIM GOD BEHOLDETH WITH A GRACIOUS EYE; PUTTETH AWAY HIS SIN BY NOT IMPUTING IT; TAKETH QUITE AWAY THE PUNISHMENT DUE THEREUNTO, BY PARDONING IT; AND ACCEPTETH HIM IN CHRIST JESUS, AS PERFECTLY RIGHTEOUS, AS IF HE HAD FULFILLED ALL THAT IS COMMANDED HIM IN THE LAW; SHALL I SAY MORE PERFECTLY RIGHTEOUS THAN IF HIMSELF HAD FULFILLED THE WHOLE LAW? I MUST TAKE HEED WHAT I SAY, BUT THE APOSTLE SAITH, "GOD MADE HIM TO BE SIN FOR US, WHO KNEW NO SIN, THAT WE MIGHT BE MADE THE RIGHTEOUSNESS OF GOD IN HIM." SUCH WE ARE IN THE SIGHT OF GOD THE FATHER, AS IS THE VERY SON OF GOD HIMSELF. LET IT BE

COUNTED FOLLY, OR PHRENSY, OR FURY, OR WHAT-
SOEVER. IT IS OUR WISDOM, AND OUR COMFORT: WE
CARE FOR NO KNOWLEDGE IN THE WORLD BUT THIS,
THAT MAN HATH SINNED, AND GOD HATH SUFFERED:
THAT GOD HATH MADE HIMSELF THE SIN OF MEN,
AND THAT MEN ARE MADE THE RIGHTEOUSNESS OF
GOD.'

VI

PAUL AS A PASTOR

IN his painstaking industry for Theophilus and
for us, Luke has provided us with an extract-
minute, so to call it, copied out of the session-books
of Ephesus. Paul had been the minister and the
moderator of the kirk-session of Ephesus for three
never-to-be-forgotten years. But he has now for
some time past been away preaching the Gospel
and planting Churches elsewhere, and another
elder of experience and of authority has all that
time sat in the Ephesian chair that the Apostle
used to occupy with such authority and acceptance.
But Paul is now coming near the end of his life.
He knows that, and he has a great longing, and a
most natural longing it is, to see his old colleagues
in Ephesus once more before he goes to be with
Christ. And thus it is that at his special request
an *in hunc effectum* meeting of kirk-session has
been called, an extract-minute of which is to be
read by the curious to this day in the twentieth
chapter of the Acts of the Apostles. Now from
this priceless little paper of Luke's we learn that,
the session being constituted, Paul immediately
took occasion to review those long past three

years that he had spent in their city, and had sat
at the head of their court. Paul had given three
of the best years of his life to Ephesus, and it was
only natural that he should take occasion to go
over those three years and look at some of the
lessons that those three years had left behind
them, both for himself and for his successors in
the eldership of Ephesus. And it is just those
fine lessons that this first of Church-historians,
with such an admirable literary instinct, and with
such sanctified industry, has here supplied us with.
Paul never spoke better. Paul simply excels himself. There is all that stateliness that never for-
sakes Paul. There is all that majesty that Paul
bears about with him at all times and into all
places. All united to a humility, and an intimacy,
and a confidingness, that always carry captive to
Paul the hearts of all men who have hearts. Paul
is simply unapproachable in a scene like this. Paul
has no equal and no second in the matters and the
manners of the heart. Paul is almost his Master
over again in these matters and manners of the
heart, so much so, that when it was all over, we
do not wonder that they all wept sore, and fell on
Paul's neck, and kissed him, sorrowing most of all
for the words which he spake, that they should
see his face no more. In no other single passage
in all Paul's Life by Luke, or in all his own
Epistles even, do we see the finished friend and
the perfect pastor as in this sederunt, so to call it,
of the kirk-session of Ephesus. This sederunt,
and this extract-minute of it, is a very glass in

which every minister and every elder may to this day see themselves, and what manner of minister and what manner of elder they are, and are not.

'Serving the Lord,' says Paul about those three years. And Paul always begins with that same thing. He begins every sermon of his, and every Epistle of his, with serving the Lord. I, Paul, the servant of the Lord, is his salutation and seal in every Epistle of his. And hence his stateliness, and hence his high seriousness, and hence his unparalleled humility, and hence his overpowering authority, and hence his whole, otherwise unaccountable, life, pastoral and all. No : the elders of Ephesus did not need to be reminded that Paul had not spent those three years serving and satisfying them. They got splendid service out of Paul, both for themselves and for their families, but all that was so because Paul did not think of them at all, but only of his Master. There was a colossal pride in Paul, and at the same time a prostrate humility, such that they had never seen anything like it in any other man ; a submissiveness and a self-surrender to all men such that as those three years went on, taught to all the teachable men among them far more for their own character and conduct than all his inspired preaching. If Paul had both forgiven and forgotten those unfortunate misunderstandings and self-assertions that will come up among the very best ministers and elders, they had not forgiven or forgotten themselves for those days, or for their part in them. And thus it was that when Paul said these words :——'Serving the Lord,' those who had known Paul best were the first to say that it was all true. Now that it was all long past, they all saw and admitted to themselves, and to one another, how in this disputed matter and in that, Paul had neither served himself, nor them, but the Lord only.

We do not at first sight see exactly why Paul should be so sore, and so sensitive, and so full of such scrupulosity, about money matters. But he had only too good cause to say all he said, and do all he did, in that root-of-all-evil matter. It was one of the many abominable slanders that his sordid-hearted enemies continually circulated against Paul, that, all the time, he was feathering his own nest. He is collecting money, they said, from all his so-called Churches, and is stealthily laying up a fortune for himself and for his family in Tarsus and Jerusalem. You all know how certain scandals follow eminent and successful men as its shadow follows a solid substance. We are ashamed, down to this day, to see Paul compelled to defend both his apostleship and himself from such tongues and such pens ; from such whisperers and such back-biters. And yet, no. We would not have lost such outbursts as this for anything, for we would never have known Paul, nor have loved him, nor have believed in him and in his gospel, as we do, had we not been present at that table beside those men who had seen Paul with all their eyes day and night for three years. I defy you ! he exclaimed, as he stood up in indignation and held

out his callid hands—I defy you to deny it. I
have coveted no man's silver, or gold, or apparel.
Yea, ye yourselves know that these hands—and as
he held them up, the assembled elders saw a
tongue of truth in every seam and scar that
covered them—these hands have ministered to all
my own necessities, and to them that were with
me. Noble hands of a noble heart!

Had his apostolic stipend been in their power
to reduce it or to increase it; had a fund for his
old age, or a legacy for his sister and her son
been at all in Paul's mind: then, in that case, he
might have been tempted to keep back some things
in his preaching, and to put some other things forward. At the same time, though considerations
of money had nothing at all to do with it, some
other matters undoubtedly had to do with it. To
me it is as clear as anything can be, that the Apostle
had been tempted, and had even been commanded,
by those very men sitting there, to keep back some
things out of his preaching that he was wont to
bring forward into it. Paul would never have said
what he did say at that heart-melting moment,
and he would never have said it with the heart-
melting emphasis he did say it, unless he had been
speaking straight to the point. It was all long
past now. He would never again either please or
displease any of those elders, or any of their wives
or children, any more. And thus it is that he
so returns upon his past temptations, and with a
good conscience toward the truth, tells them that
they may safely take all he had ever taught them

and build upon it ; for he had neither kept back
anything that had been committed to his ministry
among them, nor, on the other hand, had he
added anything of his own to it. I kept back
nothing that was profitable to you. I shunned
not to declare to you the whole council of God.
In that also there is a glass held up for all
ministers and all congregations in which to see
and to examine both themselves, and all their past
and fast-passing relations to one another, both in
the pulpit and in the pew.

'And with all humility of mind.' Evangelical
humility, as Jonathan Edwards so splendidly treats
it, lay deep down like a foundation-stone under all
Paul's attainments as a saint of God and as an
apostle of Jesus Christ. Paul's Master had taken
the proper precautions at the beginning of Paul's
apostleship that he should be all through it, and
down to the end of it, the humblest man in all the
world. By that terrible thorn in his flesh ; by a
conscience full of the most remorseful memories ;
as well as by incessant trials and persecutions and
sufferings of all conceivable kinds, Paul was made
and was kept the humblest of all humble men.
As all our preachers and pastors still are, or ought
to be. For they too have each their own thorn
in their own flesh, their own crook in their own
lot, their own sword of God in their own heart
and conscience. If it were nothing else, their daily
work is the most humiliating and heart-breaking
work in all the world. All other callings may be
accomplished and laid down; may reward and may

bring pride to those who follow them with all their might ; but never in this world the Christian ministry. And not his defeats and disappointments among his people only ; but still more, the things in a minister himself that account for and justify all those defeats and disappointments—all that makes his whole ministry to collapse, and to fall in on his heart continually, like a house that has been built on the sand. Till, whatever other gifts and graces a minister may be lacking in, it is impossible for him to lack humility. With all humility of mind, says Paul to the assembled elders of Ephesus. Humility of all kinds, he means ; and drawn out of all experiences ; and shown to all sorts of people. Till, both for a garment of office, and for a grace of character, a minister is clothed from head to foot with spiritual and evangelical humility.

' And from house to house warning every one night and day with tears.' The whole of Ephesus was Paul's parish. And, not once in a whole year, like the most diligent of us, but every day, and back again every night, Paul was in every house. Paul was never in his bed. He did not take time so much as to eat. As his people in Anwoth said about Samuel Rutherford, Paul was always working with his hands, always working with his mind, always preaching, always visiting. ' At all seasons ' are Paul's own enviable words. At marriages, at baptisms, at feasts, at funerals, at the baths, and in the market-places. Now down in an old woman's cellar, and

now up in a poor student's garret. Some men
find time for everything. They seem to be able to
manufacture time just as they need it. The sun
and the moon and the stars all stand still in
order that some men may get sufficient time to
finish their work. It is for such men that sun
and moon are created, and are kept in their places ;
they take their ordinances from such men, and
from the Task-master of such men. Paul, I
suppose, is the only minister that ever lived who
could have read Richard Baxter's *Reformed Pastor*
without going half-mad with remorse, and with a
fearful looking for of judgment. ' Another part is
to have a special care of each member of our flock.
We must labour to be acquainted with all our
people. To know all their inclinations and conversation : for if we know not the temperament or
the disease, we are likely to prove but unsuccessful
physicians. A minister is not only for public
preaching. One word of seasonable and prudent
advice will do that good that many sermons will
not do. See that they have some profitable
moving book besides the Bible in each family ; and
if they have not, persuade them to buy some small
piece of great use. If they be not able to buy
them, give them some. If you cannot, get some
gentleman, or other rich man that are willing to do
good, to do it. Another part lieth in visiting the
sick, and in helping them to prepare either for a
more fruitful life, or for a happy death.' There
are few things in ministerial history that makes my
heart bleed like the tragedy of Jonathan Edwards's

breach with his congregation, and then his banishment from his congregation. And I never can get over it that, in spite of all else, had Edwards been a pastor like Paul, that terrible shipwreck could never have taken place. And, yet, I must frankly confess, that explanation does not satisfy every case, even in my own experience. For some of the best pastors I have ever known, have been the victims of the cruellest and most heartless treachery and ingratitude, and that from some of their most pampered people.

Even the Apostle Peter makes the confession that he had found some things in Paul's Epistles hard to be understood. And so have I. And not in the Romans and the Colossians only, but almost more in this kirk-session speech of his. I can understand him, even if I cannot compete with him, in his incomparable pulpit and pastoral work. I myself go about, in a way, preaching repentance toward God, and faith toward our Lord Jesus Christ. But after I am like to drop with my work, and most of all with the arrears of it, Paul absolutely prostrates me, and tramples me to death, when he stands up among his elders and deacons and says : ' I take you to record this day that I am pure from the blood of all men !' I do not find his rapture into the third heavens hard to be understood, nor his revelations and inspirations, nor his thorn in the flesh, nor any of his doctrines of Adam, or of Christ, or of election, or of justification, or of sanctification, or of the final perseverance of the saints. It is none of all these things that I am tempted to wrest. But it absolutely passes my imagination how a horny-handed tent-maker, with twelve hours in his day, or make it eighteen, and with seven days in his week ; a mortal man, and as yet an unglorified, and indeed, far from sanctified, man, could look all his elders, and all their wives, and all their sons and daughters in the face, and could say those terrible words about their blood. Jesus Christ, who finished the work given Him to do, never said more than that. The only thing that ever I heard to come near that was when a Highland minister was leaving his parish, and said from the pulpit in his farewell sermon, that he took all his people to witness that he had spoken, not only from the pulpit, but personally, and in private, to every single one of his people about the state of their souls. Altogether, Paul was such a preacher, and such a pastor, and such a saint, that I cannot blame them for think-ing in those days that he must be nothing less than the Holy Ghost Himself, who had been promised by Christ for to come. Such was Paul's character, and such was his work, and such was his success, both as a preacher and a pastor.

With all that, and after all that is said, I am still dazzled and absolutely fascinated with Paul's pastoral work. I cannot get Paul's pastoral work out of my mind. I cannot get it out of my imagination. I cannot get it out of my conscience. I cannot get it out of my heart. Above all his other discoveries, when Professor Ramsay goes east to dig for Paul in Ephesus, I would like him to be able to disinter Paul's pastoral-visitation book. And with it the key to those cipher and shorthand entries about what he said and what he did in this house and in that, and day and night with tears. The hours he gave to it, his division of the day and of the night, the Psalms he read and opened up from house to house, the houses that made him weep, and the houses that sent him back to his tent-making singing. Did Paul make it a rule to read, and expound, and pray, in every house, and on every visit? Did he send word by the deacon of the district that he was coming? Or did he just, in our disorderly way, start off and drop in here and there as this case and that came up into his over-crowded mind? Till the learned Professor comes upon Paul's private note-book, for myself I will continue to interpret Paul's farewell address to the kirk-session of Ephesus with some liberality. Paul cannot really mean me to understand that he was always weeping, and always catechising, and always expounding, and always on his knees in the houses of Ephesus. No; Paul was Paul in all parts of his pastoral work, as well as in everything else. Paul is the last speaker to interpret in a wooden way, far less in a cast-iron way. Paul, you may depend upon it, was quite content some days just to have waved his hand in at that window, and to have saluted this and that man in the street, and to have been saluted in return by this and that gentlemanly little schoolboy with his satchel on his back. Paul would often drop in, as we say, not indeed to curse the weather, and to canvass the approaching marriages, like William Law's minister, but, all the same, to rejoice with the bridegroom and the bride, and to set down their exact date in his diary, so as to be sure to be on the spot in good time, and in his best attire. If you are a pastor, and if your visits up and down among your people help to keep your and their friendships in repair ; to re-kindle and to fan the smoking flax of brotherly love ; if your visits operate to the cementing and the stability of the congregation ; then, that is already more than one-half of the whole end of your ministry, both pulpit and pastoral, accomplished. And, with all your preaching, and with all your pastoral work performed like Paul's, in intention and in industry at least, you also will surely be able, with great humility as well as with great assurance of faith, to bid your people goodbye, and your kirk-session, saying,— And now, brethren, I commend you to God, and to the word of His grace, which is able to build you up, and to give you an inheritance among all them which are sanctified.

VII

PAUL AS A CONTROVERSIALIST

'WOE is me, my mother, that thou hast borne me a man of strife and contention to the whole earth,' complained the sorrowful prophet. And the Apostle now before us might have made that very same complaint, and with much more cause. For Paul, from the beginning to the end of his apostleship, was simply plunged into a perfect whirlpool of all kinds of contention and controversy. Wherever Paul was sent to preach ; north, south, east, and west, thither his persecutors pursued him. Till, what Jeremiah exclaimed somewhat passionately and somewhat hyperbolically concerning himself, became literally true in the case of Paul. For Paul, without any exaggeration, was made nothing less than a man of strife and of contention to the whole earth.

But, then, this is always to be kept in mind, that Paul had a splendid equipment, both by nature and by grace, for his unparalleled life of apostolic controversy. Paul started out to face that life of temptation, as nearly crucified and completely stone-dead to himself, as any man can ever hope to be in this mortal life. It is our incurable self-love that is the bitter root of all our controversies, whether those controversies are carried on by the tongue, or by the pen, or by the sword. Once slay our incurable self-love, and once plant in its place the love of God and the love of our neighbour, and you have already as good as beaten our swords into ploughshares and our spears into pruning-hooks. It is our self-idolatry and our self-aggrandisement ; it is our greed, and our pride, and our intolerance, and our contempt and scorn of all other men, that is the one and only cause of all our contentions and controversies. Now, look at Paul. You cannot read Paul's Epistles without being constantly captivated with the extraordinary geniality, courtesy, humility, simplicity, and loving-kindness, of Paul. The Apostle Paul, it has been said at the cost of a certain anachronism and anomaly of speech, was the finest gentleman that ever lived. And if we take both the etymology, and the old English usage of that term, then it may quite well be let stand as a most succinct and a most expressive description of the Apostle's character. Coleridge says that while Luther was by no means so perfect a gentleman as Paul, yet the Reformer was almost as great a man of genius. And Luther gives us a taste both of his own genius and of his own gentlemanliness also, in what he says so often about Paul. Luther is always saying such things as these about Paul. ' Paul was gentle, and tractable, and makeable, in his whole life. Paul was sweet, and mild, and courteous, and soft-spoken. Paul could wink at other men's faults and failings, or else expound them to the best. Paul could be well contented to yield up his own way, and to give place and honour to all other men ; even to the froward and the intractable. In short, Paul's unfailing gentlemanliness is his constant character in all the emergencies of his extraordinary life.' So speaks of Paul one of the most Paul-like men of the modern world. And an English gentleman, if ever there was one, has said of Paul in more than one inimitable sermon : ' There is not one of any of those refinements and delicacies of feeling, that are the result of advanced civilisation, nor any one of those proprieties and embellishments of conduct in which the cultivated intellect delights, but Paul is a pattern of it. And that in the midst of an assemblage of other supernatural excellences which is the characteristic endowment of apostles and saints.'

Now, all that arose, to begin with, out of Paul's finely compounded character by birth. After Mary, Paul's mother must surely have been the most blessed of women. And then after his birth in Tarsus there was his better birth from above. And then, with all that, there was the lifelong schooling that Paul put himself through, amid the endless trials and temptations, contentions and controversies, of his apostolic life. By all these remarkable, and indeed unparalleled, means, Paul came more and more to be of that unequalled grace of fellow-feeling with all other men, and that noble temper of accommodation and adaptation to all other men, in which he stands

out and is unrivalled at the head of all the saints
of God. Unrivalled. For no sooner has Paul come
into the same room with you, than, that moment,
you feel a spell come over you. You do not know
what it is exactly that has come over you, but you
feel sweetened, and strengthened, and happy. It is
Paul. You have never been in Paul's presence
before, and therefore your present feelings are so
new to you. For, all the time you are together,
all the time that he talks with you, and writes to
you, and even debates and contends with you, Paul
sees everything with your eyes, and hears everything with your ears, and feels everything with
your feelings. It was this that so carried all men
off their feet with Paul. It was this that made
Paul such a preacher, and such a pastor, and such
a friend, ay, and such an enemy. You could not
have resisted Paul. You could not have shut Paul
out of your heart, with all your prejudices at him,
and with all your determination never to like him,
and never to give in to him. Something like what
Jesus Christ was to Paul, that Paul was to all men.
You could not but give yourself up to Paul, he so
gave himself up to you. Origen tells us that
there were some men in the early church so carried
captive by the Apostle that they actually believed
Paul to be the indwelling Comforter Himself come
in the flesh, and come into their hearts. And
Origen confesses to having had a certain fellow-
feeling with those heretics.

Now, my brethren, to come in all this to
ourselves. For, here also, it is the old story, let

a man examine himself. Well, Paul was born a
gentleman already. Now, if you have not been so
born, yet I have heard it said that grace will make the
most unlikely of men a gentleman. I do not deny
that; only, I must say I have never known a case of
it. Tertullian has a saying to the effect that some
men are as good as Christian men already, just by
their birth of their mother. Now Paul was one of
those happy men. Paul was born with a big and
a tender heart, and divine grace had all that done
to her hand beforehand in Paul. Persecutor and all,
there was, all the time, the making of the most
perfect Christian gentleman in all Christendom in
Paul. Now, you will sometimes meet with men of
Paul's noble begetting and noble breeding among
ourselves. Not very often indeed, but sometimes.
God has not left Himself wholly without a witness,
even among ourselves. Men you cannot pick a
quarrel with even when you try. Men you always get
your own way with them. Men you always get a
soft look and a soft answer from them. Men who,
when you are a churl to them, are all the more
gentlemanly to you. Men to whom you may be
as self-opinioned and self-willed as you like, but it
takes two to make a quarrel; and, after all, you
are only one. Now, if any of you have any of that
rare original in you, bless God for it every day,
and bless all men round about you with it every day.
For there is no greater blessing to men and glory
to God in all this self-enclosed and alienated life.
But, on the other hand, if you are not naturally a
Christian gentleman, and yet truly wish to be

79

such, then, know this, that God has surpassed
Himself in fitting up and fitting out this present
life for your transformation from what you are to
what you wish to be.   I did not say that the Holy
Ghost could not make you, and make you behave
like, a Christian gentleman, both at home and
abroad.   I took care what I said.   I only said
that I had not yet made your acquaintance.

Have you ever read that completely overlaid
English classic, Paley's *Horæ Paulinæ*?   In that
incomparable specimen of reasoning the Archdeacon
has a fine expression and a fine passage on Paul's
'accommodating conduct.'   And that master of
the pen has given us in that epithet a characteris-
tically happy description of the Apostle.   For
everybody who has read about Paul at all, knows
this about him, that some of the greatest sufferings
of his life sprang to him just out of his far too
nobly accommodating conduct.   Paul cast his
pearls before swine.   Paul's sweet and beautiful
yieldingness in every matter that touched his own
opinions or his own practices, taken along with his
iron will in what was not his own ; these two
things must be taken together to know Paul.
Luther, that evangelical genius almost equal to Paul
himself, hits the whole matter here in a way that
would have delighted Paul.   'If two goats meet
each other in a narrow path above a piece of water,
what do they do ? ' asks Luther.   'They cannot
turn back, and they cannot pass each other ; there
is not an inch of spare room.   If they were to butt
at each other, both would fall into the water below

and would be drowned. What then will they do, do you suppose? What would you do? Well, Nature has taught the one goat to lie down and let the other pass over it, and then they both get to the end of the day safe and sound.' Now, Paul was always meeting goats on narrow ledges of rock with the sea below. And so are you, and so am I. And God ordains to you and to me our meeting one another in this strait gate and on that narrow way, and right below us is the bottomless pit. Will you lie down and let me pass over your prostrate body, and then we shall both be saved?

'Above all things the servant of the Lord must not strive.' So said the aged Apostle to Timothy, doing his best to put an old head on young shoulders. And I suppose every old minister who has learned anything in the school of life would say the same thing, to every young minister especially. Do not debate, said the greatest debater of his day, and one of the most masterly debaters in all literature. On no account, he said, enter into any dispute with any one, and especially about the truths of salvation. Give to all men every help to their salvation, but that of debating with them about it. And, according to my experience, William Law is wholly right. Far better let a man be demonstrably wrong in this and that opinion of his, than attempt to contradict and debate him out of it. You cannot do it. Far better a man be demonstrably ignorant in this and that even not unimportant matter, than that he be angry at you, and resentful at you, all his days, as nine out of every ten corrected and contradicted men will certainly be. You will never set a man's opinion right if you begin by hurting his pride and crossing his temper. Cross a sinner and you will have a devil, said Thomas Shepard. That may be a little too strong, but few men are angels exactly for some time after they are crossed, and contradicted, and corrected. They are joined to their idol, let them alone. Oh, but you say, So-and-so will not leave you alone. Well, my argument is not that, but this. Let you him alone. 'They say. What do they say? Let them say.' Do not you even say so much as Paul said. Do not say that their judgment is just. Santa Teresa is not one of the ladies of our Scottish covenant, but this is what she says on the matter in hand: 'The not excusing of ourselves is a perfect quality, and of great merit. It is a mark of the deepest and truest humility to see ourselves condemned without cause, and to be silent under it. It is a very noble imitation of our Lord. What about being blamed by all men, if only we stand at the last blameless before Thee!'

'Doing nothing by prejudice or by partiality,' says the Apostle, still insisting on this same matter. Now, to be absolutely free of prejudice and partiality is, I fear, not possible to any one of us in this life. But we must both learn, and labour, and pray, to be delivered from the dominion of those wicked tempers, as much as may be. This passage is five-and-twenty centuries old, but it

might have been written in London or Edinburgh
yesterday. 'No assurances, no pledges of either
party, could gain credit with the other. The
most reasonable proposals, coming from an oppon-
ent, were received, not with candour, but with
suspicion. No artifice was reckoned dishonourable
by which a point could be carried. Every recom-
mendation of moderate measures was reckoned
either a mark of cowardice or of insincerity. He
only was considered a completely safe man whose
violence was blind and boundless; and those who
endeavoured to steer a middle course were spared
by neither side.' We could all set the names of
living men, ay, and of Christian men too, over
against every line of that terrible indictment. But
the design of the great historian in publishing that
passage, as well as my design in preaching it, is to
set before you and before myself, in every possible
way, the mischief and the shame of such a state of
things. And to determine, God helping us, to
purge our hearts of all prejudice and partiality.
The best political and literary journal ever published in this country, for many years held up a
statesman of the last generation as a paragon of
every public virtue and every personal grace. All
that was noble, all that was grand and stately, all
that was truly Christian, met in that minister of
the Crown. But a crisis came when that hitherto
peerless statesman saw it to be his duty to take a
certain step in public life. And from that fatal
day, nothing he ever said or did was right. Everything in him, and everything in his party, was as

bad as bad could be. All who spoke against him in Parliament, or on the platform, or in the press, were so many Burkes come back to life. Eloquent, statesmanlike, unanswerable, were but three of the eulogistic epithets we read in every article. While, if any writer or speaker had a single word to say for that fallen idol and for his policy, they were either rogues or fools. It was a weekly lesson. And not a few of us learned the lesson. Indeed it was written so large that no one could miss learning it. It was as if it had been printed at the head of every page,—All you who would see prejudice and partiality, read what is written below. Speaking on this whole matter for myself, I owe a great debt to the conductors of that journal, and to Butler, and to Bengel. To Butler every day for that great saying of his—'Let us remember that we differ as much from other men as they differ from us.' And to Bengel for this —*non sine scientia, necessitate, amore* : enter upon no controversy without knowledge, nor without necessity, nor without love.

VIII

PAUL AS A MAN OF PRAYER

INTELLECTUALLY as well as spiritually, as a theologian as well as a saint, Paul is at his very best in his prayers. The full majesty of the Apostle's magnificent mind is revealed to us nowhere as in his prayers. After Paul has carried his most believing and his most adoring readers as high as they are able to rise, Paul himself still rises higher and higher in his prayers. Paul leaves the most seraphic of saints far below him as he soars away up into the third heaven of rapture, and revelation, and adoration. Paul is caught up so high into paradise in his prayers, that when he returns back into the body, he is not able to tell the half of the things that he has seen and heard in the presence of God. A great theologian, who is also a great devotional writer, has warned his readers against the dangers of an untheological devotion. Now, Paul's great prayers and great praises are the best examples possible of a devotion that is theological and Christological to the core. In the Ephesians and the Colossians especially, Paul's adoration flames up to heaven like the ascending incense of a great altar-fire. Paul's adorations in those two superb epistles especially, reveal to us, as nothing else of Paul's composition reveals to us, the full intellectual strength, and the full spiritual splendour, of Paul's sanctified understanding. And then those unapproached adorations of his prove this also, that the Apostle's wonderful mind has found its predestined sphere and its sufficient scope in New Testament Theology, and especially in New Testament Christology. There may have been one or two as great intellects as Paul's in some of the surrounding dispensations of Paganism; but then those greatly gifted men had not Paul's privileges, opportunities, and outlets. God did not reveal His Son in those men. And thus it was that their fine minds never had full justice done to them in this life. But in Jesus Christ, and in Him ascended and glorified, Paul's profound mind had a boundless scope and a boundless satisfaction. The truth is, beyond the best adorations and doxologies of the Apostle Paul, the soul of man will never rise on this side the adorations and doxologies of the Beatific Vision itself.

Now my brethren, there is a lesson here of the very first importance and the very first fruitfulness to you and to me. And that lesson is this. Let us put our very profoundest Christology into our prayers. One reason why so many of our prayers, both in public and in private, are so dry, and so cold, and so full of repetition, is just because there is so little Christology in them; so little New Testament Scripture, that is. I do not mean that there is too little New Testament language in our prayers; but there is too little both Old and New Testament language meditated on, understood, believed, realised, and felt. There is too little Scripture substance, Scripture strength, Scripture depth, and Scripture height, in our prayers. It was this that led Dr. Thomas Goodwin, by far the princeliest preacher of the Puritan pulpit, to counsel the divinity students of Oxford to 'thicken' both their devotions to God, and their exhortations to their people, with apostolic doctrine. Now, even if you possess no students' books of apostolic doctrine, you possess the very Apostle himself in his Epistles, and I defy you to read his Epistles with the understanding and the heart, and not to be swept away, like their writer, into the most ecstatic and rapturous adoration. You will never be able to read in that way the doctrinal parts of the Romans, and the Ephesians, and the Colossians, or, indeed, any of Paul's Epistles, without being, now completely melted and broken, and now completely caught up into paradise, till you are a second Paul yourself. If your prayers hitherto have been a weariness to yourself, and to all men who have had to do with you, and to the Hearer of prayer Himself, get Paul's great Epistles well down into your understanding, and into your imagination, and into your heart henceforth, and out of your heart, and out of your mouth, there will flame up doxologies and adorations as seraphic and as acceptable as Paul's own doxologies and adorations in his greatest Epistles.

The absolute unceasingness also of Paul's prayers immensely impresses us. In his own well-known words about himself Paul was 'praying always with all prayer and supplication in the spirit.' Now that, read literally, may well look to us like the language of a man gone into absolute exaggeration and extravagance about prayer. But it is not so. All that was literally true of Paul. Paul confessed sin for himself, and he interceded for other men; he adored also and broke out into doxologies, literally without ceasing. Do you ever employ an horology in your devotional life? You will find an excellent specimen of that apparatus and assistance to unceasing prayer on page 155 of Oliphant's edition of Andrewes's *Private Devotions.* Now just as if he had an horological tablet like that page hung up, now on his workshop-wall, and now on his prison-wall, Paul prayed night and day, and all the hours of every night and of every day, without ceasing. Like the genuine horologist he was, Paul introduced every day of his life with praise and prayer. When I awake I am still with thee! he exclaimed as he awoke. He had fallen asleep last night full of praise and prayer, and in the morning he just began again where he had left off last night. As Augustine says, Paul brought the word to the water-bason every morning and every night and made it a sacrament. Wash me, he said, and I shall be whiter than snow. I put on His righteousness, he went on, and it clothed me, it was to me for a robe and for a diadem. Thy Word—he remembered this also out of Job as he broke his morning fast—is more to me than my necessary food. And then as the day went on, every instrument he took into his hands, and every product he put out of his hands, was oratorical to Paul. Like his divine Master, everything was to Paul another speaking parable of the Kingdom of Heaven. Everything to Paul was another call to prayer and praise. Till, literally, and without any exaggeration or hyperbole whatsoever, Paul prayed and sang praises unceasingly. Until you are as old as Paul you will have no idea what a large liberty, what a rich variety, what an inexhaustible resource, and what a full range and reward, there is in prayer. What an outlet for your largest mind, and for your deepest heart, and for your richest and ripest individuality. Instead of the life of prayer being a monotony and a weariness, as we think it, there is simply no exercise of the body, and no operation of the mind, and no affection of the heart, for one moment to compare with prayer, for interest, and for variety, and for freshness, and for elasticity, and for all manner of intellectual and spiritual outlet and reward. I sometimes speak to you about Bishop Andrewes, and I do so because his *Private Devotions* is by far the best book of that kind in all the world. As also because it is never out of my own hand; and, naturally, I would like it never to be out of your hand either. And all that because Andrewes is a man after Paul's own heart, for the freshness, and for the fulness, and for the richness of his prayers. Andrewes has a Meditation for every day of the week, and an

Adoration, and a Confession of faith, and a Confession of sin, and a Supplication, and an Intercession, and a Thanksgiving, with no end of Acts of Commendation, Acts of Deprecation, Acts of Pleading, and such like. And then he has an Horology, composed exclusively out of Holy Scripture, for every hour of the day and the night. And much more of the same kind besides. What a rich, fruitful, nobly intellectual, and nobly spiritual, life Paul secured to himself, just by his habits and his hours of meditation and prayer. As Andrewes also secured in his measure. And many more who have given themselves to prayer as Paul and Andrewes gave themselves. And just because, with all that, we will not learn to pray, what a wilderness we all make this life to be to ourselves, till we lie down weary of it, and die and are buried in it. Lord, teach us to pray!

Now, just as Paul prayed always and without ceasing, so will we, if we take Paul for our master in divinity and in devotion ; and if, like Paul, we go on, in all that, to make Jesus Christ our continual atonement for our sins, and our continual sanctification from our sinfulness. If we know sin at all aright, and Christ at all aright, then this will be the proof that we do so,—we will pray for pardon and for a holy heart, literally, without ceasing. How can any man cease, for a single moment, from repentance and prayer who has a heart full of sin in his bosom, and that heart beating out its sinfulness into his body and into his mind every moment of the day and the night? That man will never cease from prayer till he has ceased from sin, any more than Paul ceased. For, with that unceasingly sinful heart within him, there are so many men, and so many things, all around him, constantly exasperating his heart. You must all know that about yourselves. You are so beset with men whom you cannot meet in the street, or hear or see their very names, but you must surely, on the spot, flee to Christ to forgive, and heal, and hide you. Those men may never have hurt a hair of your head; they will never suspect what a temptation they are to you; but such is the rooted and ineradicable malice of your heart towards them, that, as long as you and they live in this world, you will have to pray for yourself and for them without ceasing. When you cease to pray for those men, you, that moment, begin again to sin against them; and that continually drives you back to the blood of Christ both for yourselves and for them. You will never acquit Paul of having gone extravagant, and of being beside himself about prayer, till you equal and exceed him in unceasing prayer, both for yourselves and for all men. And you will so exceed him when you take your exceedingly sinful heart in your hand, and hold it in your hand, watching its motions of sin, and its need of redemption, all the day. If it were possible, and, why, in the name of God, and of your immortal soul, should you not make it possible? If it were possible, I say, to take your private diary to-morrow, and to make a cross on the page for every time you have to flee from your own heart to the blood of Christ; and then to count up the number of the crosses at the end of the day,—if you did that, 'always,' and 'unceasing,' would be the weakest words you could use about your sin and your repentance to-morrow night. On the midday street to-morrow you would stop to make those sad marks in your book, at your meals you would make them, at business, at calls, and in conversation with your wisest, and best, and least sin-provoking, friends. At your work, at your family worship, in your pew on Sabbath, at the Lord's table itself; and, if you were a minister, in your very pulpit. 'Always' and 'unceasing.' Paul made no exception, and found no discharge from that war. And neither will you, till you see Paul, and share his place with him, so close to his and your Master's feet, that sin will not reach you. An horology for one day like that would make you at night read both Paul's doctrines and his doxologies as you never read them before.

And I will be bold, and particular, and personal, at this point, and will say one thing of the foremost importance to you and to myself,—we must imitate Paul in this, and take far more *time* to prayer than we have ever yet taken. I am as certain as I am standing here, that the secret of much mischief to our own souls, and to the souls of others, lies in the way that we stint, and starve, and scamp our prayers, by hurrying over them. Prayer worth calling prayer: prayer that God will call true prayer and will treat as true prayer, takes far more time, by the clock, than one man in a thousand thinks. After all that the Holy Ghost has done to make true prayer independent of times, and of places, and of all kinds of instruments and assistances,—as long as we remain in this unspiritual and undevotional world, we shall not succeed, to be called success, in prayer, without time, and times, and places, and other assistances in prayer. Take good care that you are not spiritual overmuch in the matter of prayer. Take good care lest you take your salvation far too softly, and far too cheaply. If you find your life of prayer to be always so short, and so easy, and so spiritual, as to be without cost and strain and sweat to you, you may depend upon it, you are not yet begun to pray. As sure as you sit there, and I stand here, it is just in this matter of *time* in prayer that so many of us are making shipwreck of our own souls, and of the souls of others. Were some of us shut up in prison like Paul, I believe we have grace enough to become in that sequestered life men of great and prevailing prayer. And, perhaps, when we are sufficiently old and set free from business, and are sick tired of spending our late nights eating and drinking and talking : when both the church and the world are sick tired of us and leave us alone and forget us, we, yet, short of Blackness or the Bass-rock, may find time for prayer, and may get back the years of prayer those canker-worms have eaten.

And now to come to the last and the best kind

of all prayer, and the crown and the finish of all Paul's prayers, intercessory prayer, namely. We have little else indeed of the prayer-kind drawn out into any length from Paul's pen but prayer for other people. If you were to collect together and tabulate by themselves all Paul's prayers of all kinds, as Dr. Pope has done in his golden book, you would find that they all come in under the head of salutations, or invocations, or benedictions: intercession, in short, of one kind or other; with, now and then, such a burst of doxology as cannot be classified except by itself. What a quiet conscience Paul must have had, and what a happy heart, in this matter of intercessory prayer, compared with the most of us. For, how many people, first and last, have asked us to pray to God for them, whom we have clean forgot. How many children, sick people, heart-broken people, has God laid on our hands, and we have never once brought them to His mercy-seat. How happy was Paul, and how happy were those churches who had Paul for their pastor. How happy to have been his fellow-elder in Ephesus, his physician, his son in the Gospel. Speaking of Paul's physician, I shall close with a few lines on this subject, out of the private papers of Sir Thomas Browne, a man of prayer, not unworthy to be named with the Apostle himself: 'To pray in all places where quietness inviteth; in any house, highway, or street; and to know no street in this city that may not witness that I have not forgotten God and my Saviour in it: and that no parish

or town where I have been may not say the like.
To take occasion of praying upon the sight of any
church which I see, or pass by, as I ride about.
To pray daily and particularly for my sick patients,
and for all sick people under whose care soever.
And, at the entrance into the house of the sick to
say,—the peace and the mercy of God be on this
house. After a sermon to make a prayer and
desire a blessing, and to pray for the minister.
Upon the sight of beautiful persons to bless God
for His creatures; to pray for the beauty of their
souls, and that He would enrich them with inward
grace to be answerable to the outward. Upon
sight of deformed persons, to pray Him to send
them inward graces, and to enrich their souls, and
give them the beauty of the resurrection.' Had
Sir Thomas Browne lived in Paul's day the praying Apostle would have ranked him with Luke
and would have called them his two beloved
physicians.

Brethren, pray for me, said Paul. Pray for my
soul, said Arthur also,—

> Pray for my soul. More things are wrought by prayer
> Than this world dreams of. Wherefore let thy voice
> Rise like a fountain for me night and day.
> For what are men better than sheep or goats
> That nourish a blind life within the brain,
> If, knowing God, they lift not hands of prayer
> Both for themselves and those who call them friend?
> For so the whole round earth is, every way,
> Bound by gold chains, about the feet of God.

But that all-important matter of *time* comes back

upon me, and will not let me go.   Take more time
to prayer, my brethren.   Take one hour out of
every twenty-four.   Or, if you cannot spare an hour,
take half an hour ; or, if you would not know what
to do or say for half an hour, take a quarter of
an hour.   Take from 8 to 9 every night, or from
9 to 10, or from 10 to 11, or some part of that.
And, if you cannot fill up the time out of your
own heart, take David and Paul and Andrewes to
assist you, and to show you how to pray in secret ;
for it is a rare, and a difficult, but an absolutely
indispensable, art.

IX

PAUL AS A BELIEVING MAN

THE extraordinary concentration of Paul's faith upon the Cross of Christ is by far the most arresting and impressive thing about Paul. It is in the way that Paul lets go everything else in order that he may rivet his faith upon the Cross of Christ alone—it is this that makes Paul our model and our master in this whole matter of the Cross of Christ. For the sake of the Cross of Christ Paul denies himself daily in many other of the great things of Christ. What splendid visions of Christ there are opened up in Paul's magnificent Christology! What captivating and enthralling glimpses he gives us sometimes into the third heavens! But we are immediately summoned back from all that to be crucified with Christ. There is a time and there is a season for everything, says Paul. And I am determined, he says, that so far as I am concerned you shall know nothing in this life at any rate, save Jesus Christ, and Him crucified. A great Pauline divine, the greatest indeed that I know, was wont to say that there are many things in our Lord far more wonderful and far more glorious than even His

97

Cross. But Paul never says that. Or if he is ever carried away to say that, he instantly corrects himself and says, God forbid that I should glory save in the Cross of Christ. Like the dove to its window, like the bird to its mountain, even after he has been caught up into the third heavens, Paul hastens back to the Cross of Christ. Once Paul is for ever with the Lord; once he is sat down finally with Christ in His kingdom; once he is at home in heaven, and not merely there on a short visit; once he is completely habituated to, and for ever secure in, glory, Paul will then, no doubt, have time and detachment to give to other things in Christ besides His Cross. And yet, I am not sure. At any rate, so long as Paul is in the flesh; so long as he is still carnal and sold under sin; so long as that messenger of Satan is still buffeting him, the Cross of Christ with its sin-atoning blood is the glory that excels all else in Christ to Paul. What grapples my own heart to Paul above all else is just the unparalleled concentration of Paul's experience, and of Paul's faith, and of Paul's preaching, upon the Cross of Christ.

Another thing in Paul's faith is the extraordinary way in which he identifies himself with Christ when Christ is upon His Cross. Christ and Paul become one sacrifice for sin on the Cross. Christ and Paul combine and coalesce and are united into one dying sinner on the accursed tree. It takes both Paul and Christ taken together to make up Christ crucified. Christ is apprehended,

is accused, is condemned, and is crucified before
God for Paul ; and, then, Paul is crucified before
God in, and along with, Christ. It is this transcendent identification of Christ with Paul and of
Paul with Christ that the Apostle so labours, in
the strength and in the style of the Holy Ghost,
to set forth to us in his glorious doctrines of the
suretyship and substitution of Christ, the imputation of Paul's guilt and pollution to Christ, and
then the imputation of Christ's righteousness and
the impartation of Christ's spirit to Paul. These
great evangelical doctrines of Paul may be so
divine and so deep that your heart does not yet
respond to them. Paul's tremendously strong
words about Christ and His Cross may stagger
you, but that is because the law of God has not
yet entered your heart. When it does, and when,
after that, God reveals His Son in you, you will
then become as Pauline in your theology and in
its great language as Luther became himself. I
can very well believe that Paul's so original, so
powerful, and so cross-concentrated faith, staggers
and angers some of you. It does not stagger and
anger any of you half so much as at one time it
both staggered and positively exasperated Paul
himself. But now, he says, I am crucified with
Christ ; with Christ who loved me, and gave Himself for me. And once Paul's faith is in this way
concentrated on the Cross of Christ : and once
Paul is so identified with Christ crucified ; everything in Paul's experience—past, present, and yet
to come—all that only roots the deeper and the

stronger Paul's faith in the Cross of Christ. 1 often recall the evidence that Admiral Dougall gave at the Tay Bridge inquiry as to the direction and the force of the winds that blow down the valley of the Tay. 'Trees are not so well prepared to resist pressure from unusual quarters,' said that observant witness. 'A tree spreads out its roots in the direction of the prevailing wind.' Now Paul's faith was like one of the Admiral's wind-facing trees. For Paul's faith continually spread out its roots in the direction of the coming storm. Only, the wind that compelled Paul's faith to spread out its roots around the Cross of Christ blew down from no range of earthly mountains. It was the overwhelming wind of God's wrath that rose with such fury upon Paul's conscience out of Paul's past life. The blasts of divine wrath that blew off the bleak sides of Sinai struck with such shocks against Paul's faith in Christ, that, like the trees on the wind-swept sides of the Tay, it became just by reason of that wind so rooted and grounded in Christ crucified, that however the rain might descend, and the floods come, and the winds blow and beat upon Paul's faith, it fell not, for it had struck its roots, with every new storm, deeper and deeper into the Cross of Christ.

Down suddenly out of the dark mountains of Paul's past life of sin, the most terrible tempests would, to the very end of his days, burst upon Paul. You must not idolise Paul. You must not totally misread and persistently misunderstand Paul, as if Paul had not been a man of like passions with

yourselves. Paul was a far better believer than
you or I are. But as to sin there is no difference. And the very greatness of Paul's faith; the
very unparalleled concentration and identifying
power of his faith ; all that only made the sudden
blasts that struck at his faith all the more terrible
to bear. Oh, yes! you may depend upon it Paul
had a thousand things behind him that swept
down guilt and shame and sorrow upon his head
to the day of his death. The men and the women
and the children he had haled to prison ; the holy
homes he had desolated with his temple hordes ;
the martyrdoms he had instigated, the blood of
which would never in this world be washed off his
hands ; in these, and in a thousand other things,
Paul was a child of wrath even as others. And
that wrath of God would awaken in his conscience,
and would assault his faith, just as that same
wrath of God assaults your faith and mine every
day we live : if, that is to say, we live at all. No,
there is no difference. The only difference is
that Paul always met that rising wrath with a
faith in Christ crucified that has never been
equalled. 'I, through the law,' he said, or tried
to say, every time the law clutched at him as its
prisoner—'I through the law am dead to the
law. For I am crucified with Christ.' When
the two thieves died on their two crosses on
Calvary, ay and even after their dead bodies
were burned to ashes in Gehenna, there would still
come up to the courts of justice in Jerusalem, com-
plaints and accusations against those two male-

factors from all parts of the land. 'He stole my ox.' 'He robbed my house.' 'He burned down my barn.' 'He murdered my son.' But the judge would say to all such too-late accusations that the murderer was dead already. 'He has been crucified already. He is beyond your accusations and my jurisdiction both. He has paid already with his life for all his deeds of robbery and of blood. His death has for ever blotted out all that can ever be spoken or written against him.' And so it was with Paul. All his persecutions, and all his blasphemies, with all else of every evil kind that could come up out of his past life,—it would all find Paul already a dead man. Paul is crucified. Paul has given up the ghost. Paul is for ever done with accusers and judges both : come up what will, leap into the light what will, it is all too late. A dead man is not easily put to shame, and no jailer carries a corpse to prison. Nay, Paul's case is far better than even that of the two death-justified thieves. For, in Paul's case, two men are dead for one man's transgressions. And not two mere men, but one of them the very Son of God Himself. Truly the law is magnified and made honourable in Paul's case ! Ten thousand times more honourable than if it had never been broken, since the Divine Lawgiver Himself has satisfied the broken law, and has Himself been crucified for Paul's transgressions.

But Paul's peculiar and arresting form of speech in the text carries in it the secret of a great victory and a great peace. For mark well, what exactly

Paul says. Paul does not say that he once was, or
that he had at one time been, crucified with Christ,
but that he is, at present, so crucified. That is as
much as to say that as long as Paul has any sin
left so long will Christ be crucified. Not only is
Paul's past sin all collected up and laid on Christ
crucified ; but almost more, all Paul's present sinfulness comes up upon his conscience only to find
Paul dead to his conscience, and to his sinfulness
too, so truly and so completely is he crucified
with Christ. It is impossible properly, or even
with safety, to describe to a whole congregation
Paul's experience. But those who have this blessed
experience in themselves do not need it to be
described to them, and their own broken hearts
and holy lives are the best proof of its safety. I
will attempt to describe to some of you what
your life is, and the description will somewhat
comfort and assure you concerning it. Your heart
beats up its secret sinfulness with every pulse, so
much so, that you would choke and consume and
die with the guilt and the pollution of your heart,
unless you were dead already. As it is, though
nobody will believe it, or make sense of how it can
so be, your unspeakable sinfulness never gets the
length even of darkening your mind or imprisoning
your conscience. And that is because your mind
and your conscience are both in the keeping of
Christ crucified. As Luther's conscience was.
' The law is not the lord of my conscience,' pro-
tested that Paul-like, that lion-like, believer.
' Jesus Christ is Almighty God, and He is the

Lord of my conscience. He is the Lord of the law also, both unbroken, broken, and repaired, and He keeps the law out of my conscience by keeping my conscience continually sprinkled with His own peace-speaking blood.' In Paul's words again, the true believer is 'dead,' both to the law, and to the sin and the guilt of his own corruption. A true believer's corruption of heart comes up into his consciousness not in order to produce there a bad conscience, but in order to find the believer crucified already for all that corruption with Christ. For myself, I could not live a day, nor any part of a day, were I not crucified with Christ. I would sicken, I would swoon, I would fall down on the street, I would die. Come up beside me, my brethren! There is room in Christ crucified for us all. I am sure you live a miserable life down there, and out of Christ. It is not a dog's life down there. Come up hither to peace and rest. Learn to say, and then say it continually till you say it in your sinful dreams,—I am crucified with Christ! And then you will be able to work in peace, and to eat and drink in peace, and to go out and in in peace, and to lie down in peace, and rise up. Then you will be able to die in peace, and to awake for ever to Christ and His never-to-be-broken peace. 'I am crucified with Christ, nevertheless I live, yet not I, but Christ liveth in me, and the life which I now live in the flesh I live by the faith of the Son of God, who loved me, and gave Himself for me.'

'HIMSELF for me, HIMSELF for me!' There is

a faith that for once surely, if never again, will satisfy even Jesus Christ, and will set Him free to do some of His mightiest works. If He went about all Jewry, and all Galilee, and even crossed over into Syrophenicia, seeking for faith, surely here it is to please Him at last. The SON OF GOD for me! Surely that must go to Christ's heart, and carry His heart captive. And we also will say it; I, at any rate, will say it with Paul. For as God is my witness I feel with Paul that nothing and no one but God the Son, and God the Son crucified, could atone for my sin. The Son of God on Calvary, with all heaven and all hell let loose upon Him,—He, and He alone: He and His blood alone, can meet and make answer to the guilt and the pollution of my sin. But His blood, THE BLOOD OF GOD,—It is surely able to speak peace in my conscience and comfort in my heart: in my curse-filled conscience, and in my hell-filled heart. 'HIMSELF for me! HIMSELF for me!' For the shame, the spitting, the scourging, the staggering through the hooting streets, the bitter nails, the heart-gashing spear, the darkness of death and hell, all crowned by His Father forsaking Him,—Yes, that is the desert of my sin. That answers to my sin. My sin explains all that, and needs all that, and will be satisfied with nothing short of all that. My sin alone, in heaven, or earth, or hell, is the full justification of all that. All that, borne for me by my Maker, my Lawgiver, and my Redeemer. But it is best just as Paul has left it,—'HE loved me, and gave HIMSELF for me.'

X

PAUL AS THE CHIEF OF SINNERS

EVERYBODY knows what the most eminent saints of Holy Scripture think and say of their sinfulness. And here is what some of the most eminent saints who have lived since the days of Holy Scripture have felt and said about their own exceeding sinfulness also. And to begin with one of the very saintliest of them all—Samuel Rutherford. 'When I look at my sinfulness,' says Rutherford, 'my salvation is to me my Saviour's greatest miracle. He has done nothing in heaven or on earth like my salvation.' And the title-page of John Bunyan's incomparable autobiography runs thus: 'Grace abounding to John Bunyan, the chief of sinners. Come and hear, all ye that fear God, and I will declare what He hath done for my soul.' 'Is there but one spider in all this room?' asked the Interpreter. Then the water stood in Christiana's eyes, for she was a woman quick of apprehension, and she said, 'Yes, Lord, there is more here than one: yea, and spiders whose venom is far more destructive than that which is in her.' 'My daughters,' said Santa Teresa on her deathbed, 'do not follow my example; for I have been the most sinful woman in all the world.' But what she most dwelt on as she died was that half verse, '*Cor contritum*—a broken and a contrite heart, O God, Thou wilt not despise.' 'Do not mistake me,' said Jacob Behmen, 'for my heart is as full as it can hold of all malice at you and all ill-will. My heart is the very dung-hill of the devil, and it is no easy work to wrestle with him on his own chosen ground. But wrestle with him on that ground of his I must, and that the whole of my life to the end.' 'Begone! all ye self-ignorant and false flatterers,' shouted Philip Neri at them; 'I am good for nothing but to do evil.' 'When a man like me,' says Luther, 'comes to know the plague of his own heart, he is not miserable only—he is absolute misery itself; he is not sinful only—he is absolute sin itself.' 'I am made of sin,' sobbed Bishop Andrewes, till his private prayer-book was all but unreadable to his heirs because of its author's sweat and tears. 'It has often appeared to me,' says Jonathan Edwards, 'that if God were to mark my heart-iniquity my bed would be in hell.' 'I sat down on the side of a stank,' says Lord Brodie, 'and was disgusted at the toads and esks and many other unclean creatures I saw sweltering there. But all the time my own heart was far worse earth to me, and filthier far than the filthy earth I sat upon.' 'This is a faithful saying,' says Paul, 'and worthy of all acceptation, that Christ Jesus came into the world to save sinners, of whom I am chief.' Well may our Saviour stop us and ask us whether or no we have counted the cost of being one of His out-and-out disciples !

I can very well believe that there are some new beginners here who are terribly staggered with all that. They were brought up positively to worship the Apostle Paul, and Luther, and Rutherford, and Bunyan. And how such saints of God can write such bitter things against themselves, you cannot understand. You would like to acquiesce in all that these men say about all such matters as sin and sinfulness ; but you do not see how they can honestly and truly say such things as the above about themselves.

> Fool ! said my muse to me,
> Look in thy heart and write.

Remember these two lines of the true poet. Though they were not written about sin they never come to their fullest truth and their most fruitful application till they are taken home by the sinner who is seeking sanctification. Yes ; look well into your own heart and you will find there the true explanation of your perplexity about Paul, and Luther, and Rutherford, and Bunyan, and all the rest. For your own heart holds the secret to you of this whole matter. If you have any real knowledge of your own heart at all, this cannot possibly have escaped you, that there are things in your own heart that are most shocking and prostrating for you to find there. There are thoughts in your heart, and feelings, and wishes, and likes and dislikes ; things you have to hide, and things you cannot hide : things that if you have any religion at all you must take on your knees to Jesus Christ every day, and things you cannot take to anything even in Him short of His sin-atoning blood. Well, you have in all that the true key to Paul's heart, and to the hearts of all the rest. So much so that if you advance as you have begun you also will soon be staggering new beginners yourself with the Scriptures you read, and with the psalms and hymns you select, and with the petitions you offer ere ever you are aware ; and, it may yet be, with the autobiography you will yet write to tell to all that fear God what He hath done for your soul. Just go on in the lessons of that inward school, and you will soon stagger us all by the passion that you, as well as David and Asaph, will put into the most penitential of psalms.

'The highest flames are the most tremulous,' says Jeremy Taylor. That is to say, the holiest men are the most full of holy fear, holy penitence, holy humility, and holy love. And all that is so because the more true spirituality of mind any man has, the more exquisite will be that man's sensibility to sin and to the exceeding sinfulness of sin. 'The saints of God are far too sharp-sighted for their own self-satisfaction,' says William Guthrie in his golden little book. So they are. For, by so much the holier men they become in the sight and estimation both of God and man, the more hideous and the more hopeless do they become to themselves. Such is their more and more sharpened insight into their own remaining sinfulness. Even when God is on the point of translating them to Himself because they so please Him, at that very moment they feel that they were never so near being absolute castaways. When all other men are worshipping them for their saint-liness, and rightly so, those right saints of God are gnashing their teeth at the devilries that are still rampant in their own heart. They hate themselves the more you love them. They curse themselves the more you bless them. The more you exalt and enthrone them the more they lie with their faces on the earth. When you load them with honours, and banquet them with praises, they make ashes their bread and tears their drink. Their whole head will be waters, and their eyes one fountain of tears just at that moment when God is rising up in compassion, and in recompense, to wipe all tears from their eyes for ever.

And it is the sight of God that does it. It is the sight of Jesus Christ that does it. It is God's holy law of love entering our hearts ever deeper and deeper that does it. It is when I take my own heart, with all its wickedness-working self-love, and with all its self-seeking in everything, and self-serving out of everything and every one : with all its deceitfulness, and disingenuousness, and envy, and jealousy, and grudging, and malevolence, and lay it alongside of the holy heart of my Lord,—it is that that does it. It is then that I sit down at a stank-side with poor Lord Brodie. It is then that my midnight Bible begins to open at unwonted places, and I begin to make bosom friends of unwonted people. It is then that I search the Book of Job, say, not any more for its incomparable dialectic and its noble literature. All these things, as Halyburton has it, have now become comparatively distasteful to me. Or if not distasteful, then without taste and insipid, as Job himself says about the white of an egg. No : my soul turns in its agony of pain and shame and seeks an utterance for itself in such consummating passages as these. 'I have heard of Thee by the hearing of the ear : but now mine eye seeth Thee. Wherefore I abhor myself, and repent in dust and ashes. Behold, I am vile : what shall I answer Thee ? I will lay my hand upon my mouth.' And from that my Bible begins to open at the right places for me in David, and in Asaph, and in Ezra, and in Daniel, and in Peter, and in Paul : and so on to all Paul-like men down to my own day. And thus it comes about that the authors who are classical to me now are not the ephemerids in religion or in literature that I used to waste my time and my money upon when I was a neophyte : my true classics now are those masterly men who look into their own hearts and then write for my heart. It is the sight of God that has made them the writers they are, and it is the same sight that is at last making me the reader that I, too late, am beginning to be. It is the sight of God that does it, till my sinfulness takes such a deep spiritualness, and such a high exclusiveness, and such a hidden secretness,

that I can find fit utterance for all that is within
me in David, and in David's greatest psalms, alone.
As thus :—'Against Thee, Thee only, have I
sinned, and done this evil in Thy sight. The
sacrifices of God are a broken spirit : a broken and
a contrite heart, O God, Thou wilt not despise.
Create in me a clean heart, O God, and renew a
right spirit within me.'

It was their own sin : or to speak much more
exactly, it was their own sinfulness, that so
humbled Rutherford and Bunyan and Christiana
and Teresa, and broke their hearts. Nothing at
all humiliates; nothing really touches the hearts
of people like them ; but the inward sinfulness of
their own hearts. We shallow-hearted fools would
think and would say that it was some great crime
or open scandal that those saintly men and women
had fallen into. Oh, no ! there were no men nor
women in their day of so blameless a name as they.
One of themselves used to say that it was not 'so
humiliating and heart-breaking to be sometimes
like a beast, as to be always like a devil. But, to
be both !' he cried out in his twofold agony. The
things of this world also that so humiliate all
other men do not any more bring so much as a
momentary blush to men like Rutherford, and
women like Teresa. Just go over the things that
humilate and shame you in your earthly life and
its circumstances ; and then pass over into the
ranks of God's saints, and you will there enter on
a career of humiliation that will quite drink up
the things that make you so ashamed now, till you

will completely forget their very existence. What I am at this moment contending for is this, that sin alone truly humiliates a saint, even as holiness alone truly exalts him. It was sin, and especially sinfulness, that made those great saints cry out as they did.

A Greek fortune-teller was once reading Socrates's hands and face to discern his true character and to advertise the people of Athens of his real deserts. And as he went on he startled the whole assembly by pronouncing Socrates to be the most incontinent and libidinous man in all the city; the greatest extortioner and thief; and even worse things than all that. And when the enraged crowd were about to fall upon the soothsayer and tear him to pieces for saying such things about their greatest saint, Socrates himself came forward and restrained their anger and confessed openly and said, 'Ye men of Athens, let this truth-speaking man alone, and do him no harm. He has said nothing amiss about me. For there is no man among you all who is by nature more predisposed to all these evil things than I am.' And with that he quieted and taught and solemnised the whole city. Now in that again Socrates was God's dispensational apostle and preacher to the Greek people. For he was teaching them that there is, to begin with, no difference. That our hearts by nature are all equally evil. But that, as the Stoics taught, though all vice is equally in us all, it is not equally extant in us all. As also that he who knows his own heart will measure his own worth by his own heart and not by the valuation of the street and the market-place. As also that the noblest and best men in all lands, and in all dispensations, are those who know themselves, and who out of that knowledge keep themselves under, and wait upon God, till they attain in His good time to both a blameless heart, a blameless conscience, and a for ever blameless life.

Yet another use of this solemn subject is for the comfort of the true people of God. It is to let them see that they are not alone, and that no strange thing is befalling them, in all they are passing through. For myself, when I hear Paul saying this that is in the text, and Luther, and Rutherford, and Bunyan, and Andrewes, and Edwards, and Brodie, it is with me as it was with John Bunyan's pilgrim in the valley of the shadow of death. 'About the midst of the valley I perceived the mouth of hell to be, and it stood hard by the wayside, and ever and anon the flame and smoke, with sparks and noises, would come out in such abundance that Christian said, What shall I do? One thing I would not that you let slip. Just when he was come over against the mouth of the burning pit, one of the wicked ones got behind him, and stepped up softly to him, and whisperingly, suggested many grievous blasphemies to him, which he verily thought had proceeded from his own mind. This put Christian to it more than anything he had met with before, yet could he have helped it, he would not have done it, but he had not the discretion, neither to stop his ears, nor

to know from whence these blasphemies came.'
And here comes our point. 'When Christian had
travelled in this disconsolate condition some con-
siderable time, he thought he heard the voice of a
man, as going before him, saying, Though I walk
through the valley of the shadow of death, I will
fear none ill, for Thou art with me. Then was
Christian glad, and that for these reasons. First,
because he gathered from them that some one who
feared God was in the valley as well as himself.
Second, for that he perceived God was with them,
though in that dark and dismal state; and why
not, thought he, with me? though by reason of
the impediment that attends this place, I cannot
perceive it. Thirdly, for that he hoped to have
company by and by. So he went on, and called
to him that was before, but that he knew not
what to answer, for that he also thought himself
to be alone. But by and by the day broke.
Then said Christian, He hath turned the shadow
of death into the morning.'

XI

PAUL'S THORN THAT WAS GIVEN HIM

THE circumstances with Paul were these. To prepare Paul for his great Apostolic work he had been endowed with the most extraordinary gifts of mind. Paul was a man of genius of the very foremost rank. And nothing exalts a man, sacred or profane, in his own esteem like great genius. A towering intellect is perhaps the greatest temptation that can be put upon any mortal man. And then the unparalleled privileges and promotions that were added to all that in Paul's case, combined to make Paul's temptation to vainglory the most terrible temptation that ever was put upon any human being,—unless we call Jesus Christ a human being. But to keep to Paul. His election out of all living men for the greatest service and the greatest reward after the service and the reward of Jesus Christ Himself; his miraculous conversion; his unparalleled honours and privileges after his conversion far above all the greatest Apostles taken together; his labours more abundant than they all; and his transcending successes—all that was enough, according to Paul's own admission and confession afterwards, to exalt him above measure. Rightly received and rightly employed all these things ought only to have made Paul the humblest and the lowliest-minded of all men. But the very fact that He who knew His servant through and through saw it to be absolutely necessary to balance His servant's talents and prerogatives with such thorns and such buffetings, is a sure lesson to us that the humblest of saints is not safe from pride, nor the most heavenly-minded of men above dangerously delighting in the glory of this earth. In short, by far the best saint then living on the face of the earth was but half sanctified, and his Divine Master saw that to be the case, and took steps accordingly.

Now just what that thorn in Paul's flesh really was nobody knows. No end of guesses and speculations have been ventured about it, but with no real result. The Fathers and the Middle-age men for the most part took Paul's thorn to be something sensual, while the great body of Protestant and evangelical commentators hold that it must have been something wholly spiritual and experimental. Chrysostom thought he saw Hymenæus and Alexander in it. Whereas Calvin took it to be the lifelong impalement of Paul's inner man upon all kinds of trouble and trial. Mosheim again felt sure it was the ranklings of lifelong remorse out of Paul's early days ; and so on. In our own day interpretation has taken a line of its own on this matter. Lightfoot holds strongly that it was epilepsy. And while Dean Farrar admits that there is something to be said for epilepsy, he decides on the whole for ophthalmia. And then Professor Ramsay, Paul's latest, and in his own field one of Paul's very best commentators, has no doubt at all but that it was one of the burning-up fevers so frequent to this day in Asia Minor. Whatever his thorn really was, we are left in no doubt as to what Paul did with it. And we are left in just as little doubt as to what his Master's mind and will were about it. And then all that leads us up to this magnificent resolve of the Apostle—' Most gladly, therefore, will I rather glory in my infirmities, that the power of Christ may rest upon me.' A splendid parenthesis, in a splendid argument. An autobiographic chapter of the foremost instructiveness and impressiveness, and of all kinds of profit and delight, to read and to remember.

Now while it will be the most fruitless of all our studies to seek to find out what exactly Paul's secret thorn was; on the other hand it will be one of the most fruitful and rewarding of all our very best studies, both of ourselves and of Holy Scripture also, if we can find out what our own thorn is, and can then go on to make the right use of our own thorn. To be told even by himself just what Paul's thorn actually was would not bring to us one atom of real benefit. But if I have a thorn in my own flesh, and if I know what it is, and why it is there, and what I am to do with it—that will be one of the divinest discoveries in this world to me; that will be the salvation of my own soul to me. Never mind the commentators on Paul's thorn; no not the very best of them, lest they draw your attention away from your own. Be you your own commentator on all such subjects. Be you your own thorn-student, especially. What is it then that so tortures you, and rankles in you, till your life is absolutely intolerable to you? What is it that gnaws and saps and undermines all your joy in this life? What is it that makes you beseech the Lord thrice, and without ceasing, that it may depart from you? Tell me that, and then I will tell you Paul's thorn.

Oh, no! you exclaim to me, it was not his sore eyes. It was not his bad headaches. It was not even his frequent falling-sicknesses. Oh dear no, you say again. A thousand years of the most splitting headaches would not have laid you so low and so helpless; they would not have so taken the blood out of your cheeks, and so broken off all your interest and stake in life, and so cast you on your knees continually, as this thing has done that you point at so mysteriously, but with such evident assurance that you yourself have fallen into the same hedge of thorns with Paul. You cannot be absolutely and demonstrably sure, you admit, that it was not epilepsy, or ophthalmia, or a consuming fever in Paul. But you protest at us, as if we had been stealing Paul from you, that if it was either sore eyes, or a sick headache, or anything of that kind, then Paul was not the man that up till now you have taken him to be. But you will not let all

the world, learned or ignorant, take away Paul
from you. Almost as well take away his Master!
No! you break out with Bunyan, Paul was that
nightingale that sang his song from God to you
because his breast was all the time pressed upon
the thorn. You cannot sing like Paul, but you have
not met with any man who follows Paul's song with
more knowledge and with more enjoyment than
you do; and therefore you reason that you have
somewhat of Paul's same thorn of God against your
breast. And you speak so convincingly, and with
such a note of assurance about it, that you almost
persuade us that you have actually found out the
riddle. Only, you are almost as mysterious about
this whole matter as Paul was himself. There
are some things, you say, that must remain
mysteries, till each man discovers them for himself.
No man ever discovered and laid bare Paul's thorn
to you, and you will never open your thorn to
any man who has not already suffered from, and so
discovered, his own. You only wait till our breast
is at our thorn also; and then by our singing
you will know what has happened to us also.
When we so sing, or so listen to such singing, you
will enrol us with Paul and with yourself among
those who have come to visions and revelations of
the Lord. Oh, no! you smile at our innocence,
and say to us: Don't you see that the grace and
the strength of Christ are not prescribed anywhere
else in Holy Scripture for epilepsy or ophthalmia?
Luke was there with his balsams, and with his
changes of air, and with his rests in a desert place,

for all these ailments of the Apostle. Don't you
see, you demand of us, that this very prescription
proclaims the malady; the very medicine more
than half discovers the disease. Iron: a little
wine: sound sleep: nourishing food: a month at
the baths up among the mountains; these things
would cure the commentators. But the grace
and the strength and the righteousness of Christ
are reserved for far other thorns than Luke could
extract, or even alleviate.

It is no wonder that the most learned men
have been at their wits' end about Paul's thorn.
No blame to them since the very Apostle himself
made such a profound mistake about his own
thorn. With all his clearness of intellect, and
with all his spiritual insight, Paul was as much at
sea about his own thorn as if he had been a commentator of the dark ages. If I may say so, with
my unsurpassed respect for so great an Apostle, he
behaved like one of his own neophytes when his
own thorn first came to him from Christ. By
that time he ought to have been a teacher, but he
had still need himself to be taught which be the
first principles of personal religion, and had need
of milk, and not of strong meat. For no sooner
did the inward bleeding begin in Paul; no sooner
did he begin to lose his night's rest because of the
pain; no sooner did his heart begin to sink within
him, than he fell to praying with all his well-
known importunity that this whole thorn of his
might be immediately taken away. Greatest of
the apostles as he was; councillor almost of God

Himself as he was; Paul's insight and faith and patience wholly failed him when his own thorn began its sanctifying work within him. You never made a greater mistake yourself than Paul made. With all his boasted knowledge of the mind of Christ, there was not a catechumen in Corinth or in Philippi with more of a fretful child in him than the so-called great Apostle was when his thorn came into his own flesh. For just hear his own ashamed confession long afterwards as to what he did. Without ever once asking either his Master or himself why that thorn had been sent to him; without ever looking once into his own heart for the sure explanation and the clear justification of the thorn, he instantly demanded that it should be removed. He acted as if his Master had paid no attention as to what befell His servant. He behaved himself as if his thorn had come to him out of nothing better than Christ's sheer caprice. 'This,' he said thrice, 'is so much pure and purposeless pain. This is so much quite gratuitous suffering that Thou hast let come upon me. Let this thorn only depart from me,' he cried, 'and I will return to my faith, and to my love, and to my service of Thee and Thy people; but not otherwise. As long as this thorn lasts and thus lacerates me, how shall I serve Thee or finish Thy work?' But his Lord compassionately overlooked and freely forgave Paul all his unbelief and all his impatience and all his foolish charges, and condescended and said to him: My grace is sufficient for thee; for My strength is made perfect in weakness. Lord, exclaimed Peter in his precipitancy, not my feet only, but also my hands and my head. And Paul, a much stronger and a much less excitable man, said after he got his answer, and said it more and more all his days: 'Lord, not in one part of my flesh only, but plant those soul-saving thorns of Thine in all the still sinful parts of my body and my mind, in order that the power of Christ may rest upon me. For now as often as I am weak then am I strong. I am become a fool in my complaining. I still mistake my own salvation even when it lies at my door.'

But to come back to our riddle, and to set it over again to ourselves, so as to carry it home and work at it till we find out its true answer. What then is that thorn in the flesh of all God's best saints and of all Christ's best servants,—that thorn which still humbles, and humbles, and humbles them down, past all possible glorying in anything they are, or have ever been, or can ever be? Humbles the most heavenly-minded men in all the world down to death and hell, and so humbles such men only? What is it that Christ sends to stab His best servants deeper and deeper every day, and to impale them and buffet them till they are so many dead corpses rather than living and breathing and Christian men? And then on the other hand, what is that same thorn and stake and devil's fist that at every stab and stound and blow draws down the whole grace of Jesus Christ on the sufferer, till the sanctified saint kisses his

thorn, and blesses his Lord, and would not part
with the one or the other for all the world?
Samson offered so many sheets and so many
changes of raiment to any Philistine who within
seven days would declare his riddle. And after
John Bunyan had reset Samson's riddle to the
readers of his *Grace Abounding* he felt sure that
his sheets and his changes of raiment were all
quite safe, for, after his offer to them, he said:
'The Philistines will not understand me. But,
all the same, it is written in the Scriptures, the
father to the children shall make known in holy
riddles the deep things of God.' I give you
therefore the next seven days and seven nights,
Philistines and all, to find out Paul's great riddle.
And as many of the children of light as shall
have found out the only possible answer by this
night se'ennight shall here receive, along with the
grace and strength of Christ, a change of raiment.
Now Joshua was clothed with filthy garments, and
stood before the angel. And He answered and
said to those that stood before him, saying: Take
away the filthy garments from him. And unto
him He said: Behold, I have caused thine iniquity to
pass from thee, and I will clothe thee with change
of raiment. And I said, Let them set a fair
mitre upon his head. So they set a fair mitre
upon his head. And the angel of the Lord stood
by. Such a reward still awaits all those who so
plough with Paul's heifer as to find out his riddle.
Yes; such a beautiful change of raiment awaits
them, and such a fair mitre upon their head.

XII

PAUL AS SOLD UNDER SIN

AS often as my attentive bookseller sends me
' on approval' another new commentary on
the Romans, I immediately turn to the seventh
chapter. And if the commentator sets up a
man of straw in the seventh chapter, I immediately
shut the book. I at once send back the book and
say, No, thank you. That is not the man for my
hard-earned money. Just as Paul himself would
have scornfully sent back the same book with this
message to its author—If I have told you earthly
things, and you have so misunderstood me, how
shall I trust you to interpret my heavenly things?
No, thank you, I say, as I send back the soon-
sampled book. But send me for my student friends
as many Luthers on the Galatians as you can lay
your hands on, and as many Marshalls on Sanctification, in order that they may one day be
preachers after Paul's own heart. But no, not
that blind leader of the blind.

It is an old canon of interpretation that Paul
alone is his own true interpreter. And the true
student will take the canon down. *Non, nisi ex
ipso Paulo, Paulum potes interpretari.* That is to

say—There is no other possible interpreter of
Paul, in all the world of interpretation, but only
Paul himself. And I have come upon two other
exegetical rules that have produced the most profound results out of this present text; 'the right
context is half the interpretation.' And this out of
the same incomparable interpreter of Paul—'If a
man would open up Paul, let him do it rationally.
Let him consider well the Apostle's own words
both before the text and after it.' Now when
we take Paul in this present text as speaking
seriously and not in a sacred jest; and then
when we take the whole context, we get an interpretation altogether worthy of Paul; altogether
worthy of the depth and strength and majesty of
the Epistle to the Romans; altogether worthy of
the grace of God, and of the blood of Jesus Christ,
as, also, altogether worthy of the work of the Holy
Ghost. Then the seventh of the Romans becomes
henceforth to us, what it most certainly is, the most
terrible tragedy in all literature, ancient or modern,
sacred or profane. Set beside the seventh of the
Romans all your so-called great tragedies—your
Macbeths, your Hamlets, your Lears, your Othellos,
are all but so many stage-plays : so much sound
and fury, signifying next to nothing when set
alongside this awful tragedy of sin in a soul
under a supreme sanctification. The seventh of
the Romans should always be printed in letters of
blood. Here are passions. Here are terror and
pity. Here heaven and hell meet, as nowhere
else in heaven or hell; and that too for their last

grapple together for the everlasting possession of that immortal soul, till you have a tragedy indeed; and, beside which, there is no other tragedy. Only, as Luther says, give not such strong wine to a sucking child.

'Did I see,' says **Dr. Newman**, 'a boy of good make and mind, with the tokens on him of a refined nature, cast upon the world without provision, unable to say whence he came, unable to tell us his birthplace, or his family connections, I should conclude that there was some sad secret connected with his history.' And did I hear or read of a man of refined mind, and of a great nobility of nature that nothing could obliterate, and, withal, a truly Christian man; did I read or hear of such a man held in captivity by some vile, cruel, cannibal tribe in South America, or Central Africa, I would feel sure that he had a tale to tell that would harrow my heart. I would not need to be told by pen and ink the inconsolable agony of that man's heart. I could picture to myself that poor captive's utter wretchedness. I could see him making desperate attempts to escape his horrible captivity, only to be overtaken and dragged back to a still more cruel bondage. And were that captive able by some secret and extraordinary providence to send home to this country so much as a single page out of his dreadful life, it would scarcely be believed, so far past all imagination of free men at home would be his incoherent outcries. But all that would be but a schoolboy's story-book beside this agonised outcry of a great saint of God sold under sin.

Yes, a great saint of God. For no soul of man is sold under sin to such an agony as this who is not, all the time, a heaven-born and a holy man : holy almost as God is holy. This is the slavery of the spirit in a supremely spiritual man : a slavery past all imagination of the commonplace Christian mind. You see that in the incredulous, uncomprehending, and utterly misunderstanding way, in which Paul's agonised outbursts are sometimes stumbled at, even by some of our masters in Israel.

And no wonder, for the most complete and cruel captivity, the most utter and hopeless slavery you ever heard of, falls far short of being sold under sin. There is a depth of misery in being so sold : there is a bleak and blank hopelessness in being so sold : nay, there is a certain self-revenging admission of justice in being so sold, that all goes to make up this uttermost agony of the self-sold slave. For he was not taken in honourable battle. He was not suddenly surprised and swept away into all this terrible captivity against his own will, and against all that he could do to resist and to escape. No. The gnashing agony of his heart all his days will be because he so sold himself. This will be the deepest bitterness of his bitterest cup. This will be the cruelest rivet of his most galling chain. And then to be sold under sin ! The vilest and cruelest savage chief who makes God's earth the devil's hell to himself and others, is not sin. Sin has made him what he is, and it has made his slaves and his victims what they are; but both his cruelty and their misery fall far short of the full cruelty and the full misery of sin. Sin could bring forth ten thousand hells like that, and it could still go on bringing forth as many more. Sin is sin. And the true saint of God feels that in his heart of hearts, till he scarce feels anything else. Till what the whole life of a true saint sold under sin can be made in its agony, you may read in the seventh of Romans; unless you have such an agony in your own bosom that the seventh of the Romans sounds flat and tame beside it. 'What I hate, that do I!' Oh, no! That is no man of straw. That is no studied artifice of Pauline rhetoric. That is no young Pharisee. Oh, no, that is Paul the aged himself. That is the holy Apostle himself in all his unapproached holiness. Tragedies! Tragedies of hatred and of revenge! If you would see hatred and revenge red-hot, and poured, not on the head of a hated enemy, but, what I have never read in any of your stage-tragedies, poured in all its red-hotness in upon a man's own heart; if you would see the true hatred and the true revenge, come to this New Testament theatre. Come to Paul for a right tragic author. Or far better, come to holiness and heavenly-mindedness yourself, and then you will have this whole agony enacted in your own heart; and that with more and more passion in your heart, all the days of your life on this hateful earth. My brethren, if you will believe me, there is nothing in heaven or on earth, there is nothing in God or in man, that from my youth up I have read more about, or thought more about, than just this text and its two contexts. And if the above interpretation is not the true interpretation of this text, then I must just admit to you in the very words of St. Augustine—'I confess that I am entirely in the dark as to what the Apostle meant when he wrote this chapter.' Only, I will add this. Unless Paul contradicts me himself, not all his commentators on the face of the earth will ever convince me that this seventh of the Romans is not to be taken seriously, but is to be taken as filled with the spiritual experiences of a man of straw.

Now this is another sure rule of interpretation that whatsoever things were written aforetime were written for our learning, that we through patience and comfort of the Scriptures might have hope. And eminently to my mind the seventh of the Romans was written that those who need the very greatest patience and the very strongest comfort and consolation, may have all that here. And in this way. If even Paul was sold under sin : if even Paul when writing the Romans was still carnal : if he that very day had said and done and thought and felt what he would not if he could have helped it : if he hated himself for what came up upon him out of his heart even with his inspired pen in his hand : if sin still dwelt in him, till in his flesh there dwelt no good thing: and, then, if we delight in the law of God after the inward man, as he did : even if we find another law, as we every moment do find it, warring against the law of our mind, and bringing us into captivity to the law of sin, till we cry without ceasing, O wretched man that I am! and if all the time we thank God through Jesus Christ our Lord, and walk not after the flesh, but after the Spirit till there is therefore no condemnation to us—if all that is so, I would like you to tell me where I can find another chapter so full of the profoundest, surest, most spiritual, and most experimental, comfort. I have not found it. I do not know it, much as I need it. No. In its own wonderful way there is not a more comfortable and hopeful Scripture in all the Book of God than this. And for my part, I will not let any commentator of any school; no, not even of my own school, steal from me this most noble, and most divinely suited, cordial for my broken heart. As long as I am sold under sin I will continue to read continually this chapter, and all its context-chapters to myself, as all sent not to a man made of straw, but to a man made of sin, till he is every day sold under sin. 'It was the saying of a good man, lately gone to his rest, whose extended pilgrimage was ninety-three years, that he must often have been swallowed up by despair, had it not been for the seventh chapter of Paul's Epistle to the Romans.'

But if for the comfort and consolation of some men, this very same Scripture is written for the warning and admonition of other men. And I accordingly admonish you, as many as need this admonition, and will take it at my hands, not to flatter and deceive yourselves because you are not yet sold under sin. 'Don't speak to me,' said Duncan Matheson on the market-square of Huntly to David Elginbrod, 'I am a rotten hypocrite.' 'Ah, Duncan man,' said old David, laying his hand on his friend's shoulder, 'they never say Fauch! i' the grave.' And Holy Writ itself says that where no oxen are, the crib is clean. My brother, do not boast that you do not know what it is to be sold under sin, and that you do not believe it about Paul either. A born slave, with a slave's heart, and a slave's habits, never complains that he is a slave. He knows nothing else. He knows nothing better. He wishes nothing more than that his ear be bored for ever to his master's door. Only a free-born, and a nobly-born, man, and a man who has been carried away captive, ever cries continually, O wretched man that I am! The Talmud-men denied the sinfulness of their sinful hearts as indignantly as any of you can deny yours. And they interpreted the sixty-sixth Psalm to their scholars in the same way that some commentators interpret the seventh of the Romans. 'If I regard iniquity in my heart only, then the Lord will pass it by, and will not regard it,' so they taught their scholars.

But to return once more to the inexhaustible comfort of this text, and then close. There is no shame and no pain in all this world of shame and pain for one moment to compare with the shame and the pain of the seventh of the Romans, as you do not need me to tell you, if you have that pain and shame in your own heart. But lift up your head, for it is to you and not to any other man, that God speaks in His holy prophet and says: ' For your shame you shall have double. And for your confusion of face you shall yet rejoice in your portion. Therefore in your land you shall possess the double, and everlasting joy shall be unto you.' Agrippa was shut up in a cruel and shameful prison for Gaius's sake; but no sooner did Gaius ascend the throne than he had his friend instantly released and conferred upon him an office both of riches and renown. Moreover Gaius presented Agrippa with a chain of gold of double the weight with the chain of iron that he had worn in the prison for Gaius's sake. And so has Paul's Emperor done long ago to Paul. And so will He do before very long to you. To you, that is, who are now sold under sin for His sake. You will soon hear His voice speaking in anger to your jailors at your prison door and saying how displeased He is over all your affliction. And He will bring you forth with His own hand like Gaius; and for all your shame and pain He will bestow upon you double, with a chain of salvation round your neck that will make you forget all the sad years of your sold captivity.

> He comes the prisoners to release
>   In Satan's bondage held,
> The gates of brass before him burst,
>   The iron fetters yield.

XIII

PAUL'S BLAMELESSNESS AS A MINISTER

MOMUS himself could have found no fault with Paul. Momus found fault with everybody, with one exception. But had he lived in Paul's day Paul would surely have been a second exception to the universal fault-finding. For Paul so magnified his ministry; he so gave himself up to his ministry; he so laboured in season and out of season in his ministry; and above all he so pleased all men in all things for their good to edification; he so went about doing good and giving none offence that he lifted both his ministry and himself clear up far above all the fault-finding of all fair-minded men. So much so that Paul stands next to our Divine Master Himself as a blameless model for all ministers, as well as for all other men of God. And both his own ministry and that of all his successors were so much on Paul's mind, that in every new Epistle of his he has given us something fresh and forcible as to how all ministers are to attain to a blameless ministry, till they shall be able to give a good account of their ministry, first to their people, and then to their Master.

Now, immediately following the text and intended to illustrate and to enforce the text, Paul lays down a remarkable map; it is a whole atlas indeed of all his past ministry. A moral and spiritual atlas, that is. It is not a chartographer's atlas of all the parishes and presbyteries and synods in which Paul has lived and laboured. It is far more interesting and far more profitable to us than that. For it is nothing less than a faithful and feeling panorama of all the outstanding states of mind and passions of heart that he and his successive congregations had come through while he lived and laboured among them. The publisher of Thomas Boston's autobiography has lately given us an excellently-scaled and a most eloquent map of the parish of Ettrick. On that impressive sheet we are shown the situation of the church and the manse; the farm-towns where all Thomas Boston's elders lived who had a brow for a good cause; the hamlets also where he held his district prayer-meetings, and so on. And every inch of that minute map is a study of the foremost importance and impressiveness for all the parish ministers of Scotland. But Paul's pastoral map bites far deeper, and with far sharper teeth, into every minister's conscience than even Boston's mordant map will bite, though it is warranted to draw ordained blood also. Paul does not engrave topographically indeed all the cities, and all the synagogues, and all the workshops, in which he had lived and laboured. But he lays down with the greatest art the latitudes and the longitudes of all his trials, and temptations, and tumults as a minister. Instead of saying to us here is Philippi,

and here is Ephesus, and here is Corinth, and so
on: Paul says to us, here were afflictions, and here
were necessities, and here were troubles on every
side. And just as in Thomas Boston's parish
there are pillars and crosses set up to mark and to
record to all time in Scotland his great victories
won over himself, and his corresponding victories
won over his people; so does Paul set up this and
that great stone of ministerial remembrance and
has had these instructive things engraved upon it:
'by pureness, by knowledge, by long-suffering, by
kindness, by the Holy Ghost, by love unfeigned,
by the word of truth, by the power of God, by
the armour of righteousness on the right hand and
on the left.' There are able and devoted divinity-
students here to-night who look forward before
very long to have a church and a manse and a
pulpit and a people of their own. What would
you say, for a relaxation some day soon after the
session is over, to make a real geographical map of
all the places where Paul was a preacher and a
pastor; and then to distribute beside those sacred
sites all the afflictions, all the necessities, all the dis-
tresses, all the imprisonments, all the tumults, and
all the labours of the text. And then on the other
side of the sacred site, the pureness, the knowledge,
the patience, and suchlike, by all of which your
great forerunner and example-minister came out of
it all having given offence in nothing, but with an
everlastingly honoured name. Such an exercise,
taken in time, and laid to heart in time, would
surely help you to take in hand some hitherto

unheard-of parish in Scotland, so as to make it an Anwoth, or an Ettrick, or suchlike. There are hundreds of parishes in Scotland up to this day absolutely nameless, but to some one of which some one of you may yet marry your name for ever, till your parish and you shall shine together for generations to come, like the brightness of the firmament, and as the stars for ever and ever. You still have it in your own hands to-night to do that. But in a short time it will be too late for you also. Go, my sons, in God's name and in God's strength, determined, as much as in you lies, to give your happy people disappointment in nothing, and offence in nothing, till their children shall bury your dust in your own churchyard, amid the lamentations of the whole country-side, and shall write it over your dust that you were absolutely another Apostle Paul to them, both in your preaching of Christ crucified, and in your adorning of that doctrine.

'In tumults,' is Paul's own specially inserted expression; it is his own most feeling and most expressive description, for long periods and for wide spaces of his apostolic life. 'In tumults,' he says with special emphasis. Now we all know in what New Testament books, and in what painful chapters of those books, all those tumults are written. But it would be no profit to us to go back to-night on Paul's tumults, unless it were in order that we might the better lay our own tumults alongside of his, and lay ourselves in our tumults, alongside of Paul in his tumults. Well, then, come away, and let us do that. Come away, and let us speak plainly. What, then, have some of our tumults been, yours and mine, as minister and people, since we first knew one another? Was it Disestablishment? Was it Home Rule? Was it some heresy case? Was it the Declaratory Act? Was it the Union? Was it hymns, or organs, or standing at singing? or was it something else so utterly parochial, and petty, and paltry, that nobody, but you and I, could possibly have made a tumult out of it? Now whatever our tumult was, how did we behave ourselves in it? What are our calm thoughts about it, and about ourselves in it, now that it is all over? However it may be with you and me, it is certain that some men have gone to judgment, out of those very same tumults, with everlasting shame on their heads. How then do we stand in this matter of blame and shame? And blame and shame or no, are we any wiser men, and any better men to-day because of those tumults? Or after all our lessons are we just as ready for another tumult, and as ill-prepared for it as ever we were? Are we just as ill-read, and as ill-natured, and as prejudiced, and as hot-headed, and as full of pride and self-importance, as ever we were? What do you think? What do you feel? What do you say? You must surely see now, as you look back, what a splendid school for Christian character, and for Christian conduct, all those tumults were fitted, and were intended of God, to be to you. Well then, how do you think you have come out of those great years in those great and costly schools? Has your temper and your character come out of those terrible furnaces like gold tried in the fire? For, all those tumults, whatever you may have made of them, and they of you, they were all intended to be but means to a far greater end than their own end. That is to say, they were all intended to test and try and prove you and me as both ministers and men of God, and that by the only proof we can give to God or man. The proof, that is, of patience, and purity of motive, and sufficient knowledge, and long-suffering, and love unfeigned, and the word of truth, and the power of God. And to show to all men, as Paul did, that we have not received the grace of God in vain; because, amid our greatest tumults, we have given offence in nothing, and in nothing has our ministry been to be blamed.

My brethren, you are not ministers, thank God for that. But you will let your ministers tell you what is in their hearts concerning you, and concerning themselves, as they read this too proud chapter of Paul's. If you were all ministers I would go on to say in your name, and you would agree with me, as to what a cruel chapter this is. For once—what a heartless chapter! Was it not enough for Paul that he should enjoy his own good conscience as a minister, but he must make my conscience even more miserable than it was before? What delight can it give him to pour all this condemnation and contempt upon me and

my ministry? Did he not know, did he not take
time to consider, that he was trampling upon
multitudes of broken hearts? I wonder at Paul.
In so scourging the proud-hearted and uplifted
Corinthians he must have forgotten all us poor
ministers, who, to all time, would read his blameless and boasted ministry, only to be utterly
crushed by it. It was not like Paul to glory over
us in that way. But let us recollect ourselves, and
say that it is all right. It is not for such as we
are to be puffed-up, or even to be easy-minded, or
to be anything else but bruised, and broken, and
full of the severest self-blame. And, therefore,
we will go back upon the ruins of our ministry
with this self-condemning chapter in our hands,
and will recall the tumults that so wounded the
Church of Christ, and so many hearts in her, and
all the unpardonable part we took in those
tumults, that would never have been what they
were had we not been in them. Our offences
without number also in our very pulpits. Oh, my
brethren, the never-to-be-redeemed opportunities
of our pulpits; and the lasting blame of God and
our people, and our own consciences, for our
misuse and neglect of our pulpits! Rock of
Ages, cleft for ministers! The 'unedifying con-
verse' of our pastorate, and so on: till we take
up this terrible chapter, and read it continually,
deploring before God and man, to our dying day,
all that Paul was, and that we were not: and all
that he was not, and that we were. But, with all
that is for ever lost, there is one thing left that

we shall every day do; and a thing that Paul did not do, on that day at any rate, when he wrote this proud chapter. We shall every day walk about amid the ruins of our past ministry, and shall say over it—Out of the depths have I cried unto Thee, O Lord. If Thou, O Lord, shouldest mark iniquity, O Lord, who shall stand! Deliver me from blood-guiltiness, O God, Thou God of my salvation; then will I teach transgressors Thy ways; and sinners shall be converted unto Thee. There is always that left to us, and that is better for us, and far more becoming in us, than the most blameless ministry.

Thomas Goodwin, that great minister, tells us that always when he was tempted to be high-minded and to forget to fear, he was wont to go back and take a turn up and down in his unregenerate state. Now, your ministers do not need to go so far back as that. All that we need to do is to open a few pages of our communion-rolls and visiting-books, and a short turn up and down those painful sheets, with some conscience, and some heart, and some imagination, will always make high-mindedness, and self-esteem, for ever impossible to us. You do not need to keep up our faults and failures and offences against us, for we never forget them for a single day. You may safely forgive us, for we shall never in this world forgive ourselves. How could we? No other man can possibly have such a retrospect of faults and failures and offences as a minister. It is impossible. The seventh of the Romans has been called the greatest tragedy that ever was written in Greek or in English. If that is so, some of our communion-rolls and pastoral-visitation books are not far behind it. For the supreme tragedy of his own sad ministry is all written there by each remorseful minister's own hand. And such tragic things are written, or, rather, are secretly ciphered there, as to raise both pity, and fear, and terror, to all ministers, enough to suffice them for all their days on earth.

Now, you may well think that Paul has left nothing at all for you to-night, but for ministers only. Well, take this, as if Paul himself had said it. Find as little fault with your ministers as is possible. Blame them as little as you can, even when they are not wholly blameless. It is not good for yourself to do it, and it is not good for your children to hear you doing it. Be like Bacon's uncle with his family : reprehend them in private and praise them in public. That is to say, if you have a minister who will take reprehension, either in public or in private, at your hands. But, even when it must be done, do it with regret and with reverence. Be careful not to humiliate your minister overmuch. I am sure you will never intentionally insult him, however much you may have to remonstrate with him. I admit that this lesson is not literally within the four corners of the text, but it is not very far away from it.

And there is this also about offences, and fault-findings, and in a far wider field than the ministry merely. It is very humbling, when once we begin to discover it, that our very existence is an offence to so many men. We are like a stumbling-stone in their way: they fall on us and are broken, even when they could not explain or justify why that should be so; while sometimes, again, our offensiveness will only be too easily explained both to them and to ourselves. But, at other times, they will need to go down into their own hearts for the real root of all this bitterness. And, then, when they do that, you will not be much more troubled with your offensiveness to them, or with their hostility to you. At the same time, walk you softly, as long as you are in this life. It is a dreadful thing to be the cause, guilty or innocent, of another man's stumbles and falls. 'Love to be well out of sight,' was the motto of more than one of the great saints. And, though that does not sound at first sight like great saintliness, yet it is. There are few better evidences of great and sure saintship, than just to 'seek obscurity' for such reasons as the above. Keep out of people's eyes, and ears, and feet, and tongues then, as much as you can, and as long as you continue to cause so many men to stumble, and to fall, and to be broken over you.

And, then, both ministers, and all manner of men, never allow yourselves to answer again, when you are blamed. Never defend yourself. Let them reprehend you, in private or in public, as much as they please. Let the righteous smite you: it shall be a kindness: and let him reprove you:

it shall be an excellent oil, which shall not break your head. Never so much as explain your meaning, under any invitation or demand whatsoever. They just wish to pick a quarrel with you, and you have something else to do. Now, I always like to seal down such a great lesson as this by some great name. A great name impresses the most hardened hearer. And I will seal down this great lesson by this out of a truly great name. 'It is a mark of the deepest and truest humility,' says a great saint, 'to see ourselves condemned without cause, and to be silent under it. To be silent under insult and wrong is a very noble imitation of our Lord. O my Lord, when I remember in how many ways Thou didst suffer detraction and misrepresentation, who in no way deserved it, I know not where my senses are when I am in such a haste to defend and excuse myself. Is it possible I should desire any one to speak any good of me, or to think it, when so many ill things were thought and spoken of Thee! What is this, Lord: what do we imagine to get by pleasing worms, or by being praised by creeping things! What about being blamed by all men, if only we stand at last blameless before Thee!'

XIV

PAUL AS AN EVANGELICAL MYSTIC

THE two words 'mystical' and 'mysterious'
mean, very much, the same thing. Not
only so, but at bottom 'mystical' and 'mysterious'
are very much the very same words. Like two
sister stems, these two expressions spring up out
of one and the same seminal root. Now, as to
mysticism. There are more kinds of mysticism
than one in the world. There is speculative
mysticism, and there is theosophical mysticism,
and there is devotional mysticism, and so on. But
to us there is only one real mysticism. And that
is the evangelical mysticism of the Apostle Paul.
And that mysticism is just the profound mysteriousness of the spiritual life, as that life was first
created by the Holy Ghost in Jesus Christ, and
will for ever be possessed by Jesus Christ as His
own original life; and then as it will for ever be
conveyed from Him down to all His mystical
members.

Now, to begin with, Christ Himself is the great
mystery of godliness. Almighty God never
designed nor decreed nor executed anything in
eternity or in time, to compare, for one moment,

149

for mysteriousness, with Christ. All the mysteries of creation,—and creation is as full as it can hold of all kinds of mysteries: all the mysteries of grace, — and grace is full of its own proper mysteries also: yet, all are plain and easy to be understood, compared with the all-surpassing mystery of Christ. Ever since Christ was set forth among men the best intellects in the world have all been working on the mystery of Christ. And, though they have found out enough of that mystery for their own salvation, yet they all agree to tell us that there are heights and depths of mystery in Christ past all finding out. Christ, then, that so mysterious Person who fills the Gospels and the Epistles with His wonderful words and works,—What think ye of Christ? Paul tells us in every epistle of his what he thinks of Christ, and it is this deep, spiritual, experimental, and only soul-saving, knowledge that Paul has of Christ, it is this that justifies us in calling him the first and the best of all mystics; the evangelical and true mystic: the only mystic indeed, worthy, for one moment, to bear that deep and noble name.

When you take to reading the best books you will be sure to come continually on such strange descriptions and expressions as these: Christ mystical; Christ our mystical Head; Christ our mystical Root; the mystical Union of Christ with all true believers; the mystical Identity of Christ with all true believers, — and suchlike strange expressions. But, already, all these deep doctrines and strange expressions of evangelical mysticism are to be found in the deep places of Paul: and, in his measure, in the deep places of John also; and that because those two apostles, first of all spiritually-minded men, discovered all these mysterious and mystical matters in their Master. Ere ever we are aware we ourselves are mystics already as soon as we begin to read in John about the Living Bread, and the True Vine; and in Paul about the Head of the Church and His indwelling in us. But Paul, after his grand manner, goes on to show us that Christ is not the only mystical Head that this so mystically-constituted world of ours has seen. First and last, as that great evangelical and speculative mystic has had it revealed to him, there have been two mystical Heads set over the human race. Our first mystical Head was Adam, and our second mystical Head is Christ. Speaking mystically, says the most mystical of the Puritans, there are only two Men who stand before God; the first and the second Adam; and these two public Men have all us private men hanging at their great girdles. But, all the time, above Adam, and before Adam, and only waiting till Adam had shipwrecked his headship and all who were in it with him, stood the second Adam ready to restore that He had not taken away. And Paul so sets all that forth in doctrine, and in doxology, and in gospel invitation and assurance, that the Church of Christ in her gratitude to Paul has given him this great name of her first and her most evangelical mystic. 'And hath put all things under

His feet,' proclaims the great mystic, ' and gave
Him to be the Head over all things to the Church,
which is His body.' And again, ' Him which is
the Head, even Christ, in whom the whole body
maketh increase unto the edifying of itself in love.'
And again, ' And He is the Head of the body :
for it pleased the Father that in Him should all
fulness dwell.'

But while Paul has many magnificent things to
teach us about the mystical Headship of Christ
over His Church, at the same time, it is the
mystical union of Christ with each individual
believer, and each individual believer's mystical
union with Christ,—it is this that completes and
crowns Paul's evangelical doctrine and kindles his
most rapturous adoration. And all that is so,
because all Paul's preaching is so profoundly
experimental. Paul has come through all that he
preaches. Goodwin, that so mystical and so
evangelical Puritan, says that all the ' apostolical
and primitive language was at once mystical and
experimental.' But there is a more primitive and
a more experimental and a more mystical language
than even the apostolical. ' I am the bread of
life : he that cometh to Me shall never hunger ;
and he that believeth in Me shall never thirst.
This is the bread that cometh down from heaven,
that a man may eat thereof and not die. Verily,
verily, I say unto you, except ye eat the flesh of
the Son of Man and drink His blood, ye have no
life in you.' As also in our Lord's so mystical
and so beautiful parable of the true vine and its

true branches. And then in the next generation, Paul comes forward with his own so profound experience of all that, and with his own so first-hand witness to all that, in such sealing and crowning testimonies and attestations as these :—
'I live, yet not I, but Christ liveth in me : and the life I now live in the flesh, I live by the faith of the Son of God.' And, again, 'To me to live is Christ, and to die is gain,' and so on in all his epistles. Paul has so eaten the flesh and has so drunk the blood of Christ : he has been of the Father so engrafted into Christ, that he possesses within himself the very same life that is possessed by the risen Christ. The very identical life that is in Christ glorified is already in Paul, amid all his corruptions, temptations, and tribulations. There are very different degrees of that life, to be sure, in Christ and in Paul ; but it is the very same kind of life. There is not one kind of spiritual life in Christ, and an altogether different kind of spiritual life in Paul. The same sap that is in the vine is in the branch. The same life that is in the head is in the member. But that is not all. Amazing as all that is, that is far from being all. The riches that are treasured up in Christ are absolutely unsearchable. For Paul is not content to say that he has in his own heart the identical and very same life that is in Christ's heart : Paul is bold enough to go on to say that he actually has Christ Himself dwelling in his very heart. I,—you and I,—have in our hearts the very same life that was in Adam, with all its

deadly infection and dreadful pollution; but, identified with Adam as we are, Adam does not really and actually dwell in our hearts. We still inherit the 'fair patrimony' that he left us; but, I for one, both hope and believe, that Adam has escaped that patrimony himself. At any rate, wherever Adam dwells, he does not dwell in our hearts. But the second Adam is so constituted for us, and we are so constituted for Him, that He, in the most real and actual manner, and without any figure of speech whatever, dwells in us. Indeed, with all reverence, and with all spiritual understanding, let it be said, Christ has no choice; He has nowhere else to dwell. If Christ is really to dwell, to be called dwelling, anywhere, it must be in Paul's heart, and in your heart, and in my heart. Christ is so mystical and mysterious: He is so unlike any one else in heaven or earth: He is such an unheard-of mystery, that He has *three* dwelling-places. To begin with, He is the Son of God; and as the Son of God He dwells in the Father, and the Father in Him. And, then, ever since His Incarnation, He has been the Son of Man also. And as the Son of Man, and ever since His ascension and reception, He has dwelt in heaven as one of God's glorified saints, and at the head of them. But, over and above being both Son of God and Son of Man: from the mystical union of the Godhead and the Manhood in His Divine Person, He is the Christ also. And as He is the Christ, He dwells in His people, and can dwell nowhere else, in heaven or in earth, but in His people. Christ mystical is made up not of the Head only, but of the Head and the members taken together. And, as apart from · the Head the members have no life ; so, neither apart from His members has the Head anywhere to dwell. Nay, apart from His members, the Head has no real and proper existence. At any rate, as Paul insists, they are His fulness, and He is complete in and by them ; just as they again are complete in and by Him. Paul, and you, and I, hung, originally, and in the beginning, at Adam's mystical girdle, and we have all had to take the consequences of that mystical suspension. But now we have all been loosened off from Adam, and have been united close and inseparably to Christ. Before God, we all hang now at Christ's mystical girdle. Ay, far better, and far more blessed than even that, Christ now dwells under our girdle, and dwells, and can dwell, nowhere else. That is to say, in simple and plain language, He dwells in our hearts by faith and love on our part, and by mystical incorporation on His part. I am crucified with Christ, nevertheless I live ; yet not I, but Christ liveth in me. And, for this cause, I bow my knees unto the Father of our Lord Jesus Christ, that Christ may dwell in your hearts by faith.

Now, as might be looked for, a thousand things, mystical and other, follow from all that, and will, to all eternity, follow from all that. But take one or two things that immediately and at once follow from all that, and so close this meditation.

And first, the mystical union between Christ and the soul is so mysterious that it is a great mystery even to those who are in it, and share it. As Walter Marshall, one of the greatest doctors in this mystery, has it : 'Yea,' says Marshall in his *Gospel Mystery*, 'though it be revealed clearly in the Holy Scriptures, yet the natural man has not eyes to see it there. And if God expresses it never so plainly and properly, he will still think that God is speaking in riddles and parables. And I doubt not but it is still a riddle, even to many truly godly men, who have received a holy nature from God in this way. For the apostles themselves had the saving benefit of this mystery long before the Comforter had discovered it clearly to them. They walked in Christ as the way to the Father, before they clearly knew Him to be the way. And the best of us know this mystery but in part, and must wait for the perfect knowledge of it in another world.' So mysterious is this mystery of godliness.

But how, asks some one honestly and anxiously, —how shall I ever become such a miracle of divine grace as to be actually, myself, a member of Christ's mystical body ? Just begin at once to be one of His members, and the thing is done. Your hands do not hang idle and say,—How shall we ever do any work ? Your feet do not stand still and say,—How shall we ever walk or run ? Nor your eyes, nor your ears. They just begin to do, each, their proper work, and the moment they so begin, your head and your heart immediately send down their virtue into your hands and your feet. And so is it with the mystical Head and His mystical members. Just begin to be one of His members, and already you are one of them. Believe that you are one of them, and you shall be one of them. Just think about Christ. Just speak to Christ. Just lean upon, and look to Christ. Just go home to-night and do that deed of love, and truth, and humility, and brotherly-kindness, and self-denial, in His name, and, already, Christ is dwelling in you, and working in you as well as in Paul. Saul of Tarsus just said as he lay among his horse's feet,— Lord, what wilt Thou have me to do? and from that moment the thing was done.

Now, my brethren, if I have had any success to-night in setting forth Paul as an evangelical mystic, this also will follow as one of the many fruits of my argument. This fine word 'mystical' will henceforth be redeemed in all your minds from all that dreaminess, and cloudiness, and unreality, and unpracticalness, with which it has hitherto been associated in your minds. 'Vigour and efficacy' may not have been associated in many minds with the great mystical saints, and yet that is the very language that is used concerning them by no less an authority than Dr. Johnson. But just look at two or three of the greatest evangelical and saintly mystics for yourselves, and see if the great critic and lexicographer is not literally correct. Where is there vigour and efficacy in all the world like the vigour and efficacy of the Apostle Paul? Where is there less dreaminess or less cloudiness

than in Paul? What a leader of men he was!
What a founder and ruler of churches! What a
man of business he was, and that just because of
his mystical oneness with Christ. What an incomparably laborious, efficient, and fruitful life Paul
lived! What a mystical conversation with heaven
he kept up, combined with what stupendous
services on earth! Take Luther also. There is
not a more evangelically-mystical book in all New
Testament literature than Luther's Galatians.
And yet, or I should rather say, and therefore,
what truly Pauline vigour and efficacy in everything! And take Teresa and her mystical deacon
always at her side, John of the Cross. I would
need to be a genius at coining right words before I
could describe aright to you that amazing woman's
statesmanship and emperorship in life and in
character. Founding schools, selecting sites,
negotiating finances, superintending architects and
builders and gardeners; always in the kitchen,
always in the schoolroom, always in the oratory,
always on horseback. A mother in Israel. A
queen among the most queenly women in all the
world. And, unjust as Dr. Duncan is to William
Law our greatest English mystic, Duncan is compelled to allow about Law that 'he spoke upon
the practical as with the sound of a trumpet. In
practical appeals Law is a very Luther. Luther
and Law were Boanerges.' And, as Dr. Somerville
says, from whose fine book on Paul I have borrowed
the title of this lecture:—'The intensity that
characterised the religious life and experience of

the late General Gordon, was all due to his evangelical mysticism. All associated in his case also with extraordinary efficiency in the practical affairs of life and in the management of men.' But why argue out such remote and historical instances when we have it all within ourselves? Let any man among ourselves carry about Christ in his own heart; let any man abide in Christ as the branch abides in the vine : let any man cleave as close to Christ as a member of our body cleaves close to its head : let any man say unceasingly every day, and in every cross and temptation of every day, 'I am crucified with Christ : nevertheless I live : yet not I, but Christ liveth in me'; and you will be absolutely sure to find that man the most willing, the most active, the most practical, and the most efficient man in every kind of Christian work. In one word, the more evangelically mystical any man is, the more full of all vigour and all efficacy will that man be sure to be.

XV

PAUL'S GREAT HEAVINESS AND CON-
TINUAL SORROW OF HEART

PAUL'S all-but complete blindness to the beauties of nature and to the attractions of art, as well as his all-but absolute indifference to the classic sites and scenes of Greece and Rome, has been often remarked on, and has been often lamented over. Paul's utter insensibility has been often set in severe contrast over against our Lord's much-applauded love of nature. Calvin also has suffered no little vituperation for sitting all day over his Institutes, and never once lifting up his eyes to give us a description of the Alps overhead. The prince of Scripture commentators will never be forgiven for never having once stood up in rapture over the sun-risings and the sun-settings on the Alpine snows. Pascal also has come under the same condemnation because he could see no scenery anywhere much worth wondering at outside the immortal soul of man. And we are all at one in despising and spurning St. Bernard because he rode a whole day along the shores of the lake of Geneva with his monk's cowl so drawn down over his eyes that he had to ask his host at sunset where that famous water was which he had heard so many people talking so much about. Now, I am not going to put forward any defence or excuse of mine for Paul's limitations and insensibilities. The very most I shall attempt to do is to offer you some possible explanation of that great heaviness of mind, and that great sorrow of heart, which has lost Paul the full approval of so many of his best friends. How was it possible for Paul to travel through those so famous scenes, how was it possible for him to live in those so classic cities, and never to give us a single sentence about persons and places, the very names of which make our modern hearts to beat fast in our bosoms to this day?

> In vain to me the smiling mornings shine,
>   And reddening Phœbus lifts his golden fire;
> The birds in vain their amorous descant join,
>   Or cheerful fields resume their green attire.
> These ears, alas! for other notes repine;
>   A different object do these eyes require;
> My lonely anguish meets no heart but mine,
>   And in my breast the imperfect joys expire.

Right or wrong; praise Paul or blame him; try to understand him, and to feel with him and for him, or no; the thing is as clear as day, that some iron or other has so entered Paul's soul, and an iron such, that it will never depart from his soul in this world. And, till that rankling spear-head, so to call it, is removed for ever out of Paul's mind and heart in another world than this, say what you will to blame Paul, he has no ear left for the singing of your amorous birds, and no eye left but for that holy whiteness that so stains to his eyes both Mount Salmon and Mont Blanc. Master, said the holiday-minded disciples, see what manner of stones, and what buildings are here. But He turned and said to the twelve, I have a baptism to be baptized with, and how am I straitened till it be accomplished. The immense size of those stones, and the exquisite carving of their capitals, would have interested Him at another time, but His own time was now at hand: and so much so that He could see nothing else, all that terrible week, but Gethsemane and its cup, and Calvary and its cross. And, to come down to His great servant: when Mont Blanc was so full to him of the glory of snow and sunshine on many a Sabbath morning, Calvin was wont to boast it all back into its own place with this out of the Psalms,—'The hill of God is as the hill of Bashan; an high hill as the hill of Bashan. Why leap ye, ye high hills? This is the hill that God desireth to dwell in: yea, the Lord will dwell in it for ever'; and, so singing, Calvin went up again to Mount Zion. Cicero says somewhere that Plato and Demosthenes, Aristotle and Socrates, might have respectively excelled in each other's province, had it not been that each one of those great men was so absorbed in his own province. And Paul might have been a Christian Herodotus, and a New Testament Pausanias, had it not been for his own

absolutely absorbing province of sin and salvation
from sin.

> All thoughts, all passions, all delights:
> Whatever stirs this mortal frame;
> All are but ministers of Love,
> And feed His sacred flame.

Among all the heathenish doxologies of her
voluminous devotees, nature has never had half
such a noble tribute paid to her true greatness, as
Paul pays to her, in three verses of his immortal
eighth chapter. All the true lovers of nature:
that is to say, all the true worshippers, not of
nature, but of Jesus Christ; have by heart, and
have deep down in their heart, that famous but
wholly unfathomable tribute. Listen to nature's
truest prophet, and truest priest, and truest poet,
the Apostle Paul. 'For the earnest expectation
of the creature waiteth for the manifestation of
the sons of God. For the creature was made
subject to vanity, not willingly, but by reason of
Him who hath subjected the same in hope. Because the creature itself shall be delivered from
the bondage of corruption into the glorious liberty
of the sons of God. For we know that the whole
creation groaneth and travaileth in pain together
until now. And not only they, but ourselves
also, which have the first-fruits of the Spirit, even
we ourselves, groan within ourselves, waiting for
the adoption.' Match that, if you can, for a
tribute to nature's true greatness. Match that, if
you can, out of all your sentimental stuff. You
cannot do it. I defy you to do it. Pascal is

constantly saying this of man, that man's great misery is the true measure of his greatness. Give me, therefore, Paul's profound lamentation over the bondage, and the vanity, and the groaning, and the travailing of nature; and over the shame, and the sin, and the misery of man her master. And, then, give me his magnificent prophecy over her evangelical future. To all of which profound pathos on the one hand, and to all of which magnificent hope on the other hand, your nature-worshipper's unbroken heart is utterly stupid and dead. Paul was such a great man, and such a great apostle of the Creator and Redeemer both of man and of nature, that, in their present state of sin and misery, and on that account, like his Master, he was a man of inconsolable sorrows. And yet babes at the breast will wail out against the insensibility of that mighty mind and mighty heart; will wail out at his insensibility and indifference to those toys and trifles that so sanctify and satisfy them, as they so often assure us. Whatever may be the true explanation of your entire satisfaction with nature, and with art, and with travel, and with yourself, this is undoubtedly the true explanation of Paul's great heaviness and continual sorrow of heart. The tremendous catastrophe of the fall of man, and the fall of all nature around man,—that, to Paul, was so ever-present and so all-possessing, that there is no alleviation of his awful pain of heart on account of all that. At any rate, there is no alleviation or relief for him in the colour of the morning or evening sky, or in the shape of the hills, or in the music of the woods and the waters. Miserable comforters are all these things to Paul's broken heart; but, most miserable of all, your mountebank comforters among men, who would thrust things like these upon Paul's profound and inappeasable sorrow. 'A man in distress,' says John Foster, 'has peculiarly a right not to be trifled with by the application of unadapted expedients: since insufficient consolations but mock him, and deceptive consolations betray him.' The whole truth about Paul, above all other mortal men, is this. Paul is so intensely religious in his whole mind, and heart, and imagination, and temperament, and taste: he is so utterly and absolutely godly; he is such an out-and-out Christian man and Christian apostle: he is so consumed continually with his hunger and his thirst after righteousness: he is so captivated, enthralled, and enraptured with the beauty of holiness, that nothing will ever satisfy Paul, either for nature, or for art, or for travel, or for man, or for himself, short of the new heavens and the new earth. And until that day dawns, and that day-star arises in Paul's heart, whatever you and I may do, he will continue to look, not at the things that are seen, but at the things that are not seen; for the things which are seen are temporal, but the things which are not seen are eternal. Renan sometimes hits the mark in a manner that both surprises and rebukes us. 'Paul,' says that truly wonderful writer, 'belongs wholly to another world than this present

world. Paul's Parnassus and Olympus; his sunrises
and his sunsets; his whole Greece, and Rome, and
Holy Land itself, are all elsewhere, and not here.'

But not amidst nature and art and travel only,
but amidst far better things than these, men like
Paul are often made men of sorrow and of a heavy
heart. 'How, now, good friend, whither away
after this burdened manner? A burdened manner
indeed, as ever I think poor creature had. Hast
thou a wife and children? Yes; but I am
so laden with this burden, that I cannot take
that pleasure in them as I once thought I would.
Methinks, I am as if I had them not.' A bold
passage, but a right noble passage. A Paul-like
passage. Paul had neither wife nor child, but he
could not have written a better passage than John
Bunyan's above passage, even if he had had as
many children as John Bunyan had, and had loved
them, and had wept over them, as only John
Bunyan could love and weep. At the same time,
it would have been an additional relief, and a real
and a peculiar support to us, to have had a passage
immediately from Paul's own pen on the heaviness
of heart that cannot but accompany family life,
when a man of Paul's sensibility, and of John
Bunyan's sensibility, is at the head of that family.
For Paul's most noble lamentation over the out-
of-doors creation is cold and remote, and is wholly
without those bowels and mercies, that would have
been stirred in Paul had he walked with a perfect
heart before his house at home. But in the
absence of Paul on the profoundest aspects of

family life, I know nothing better anywhere than the Pilgrim's reply to Mr. Worldly Wiseman; and, some time after, to Charity. To Charity, who, though like the Apostle she has no children of her own body, yet like him, her love, and her imagination, and her genius for the things of the heart, all make her speak to us like a mother in Israel, and all make John Bunyan to speak in reply to her like a father in the same. As Thomas Boston also has it in one of his Shakespearian passages: 'Man is born crying, lives complaining, and dies disappointed from that quarter. All is vanity and vexation of spirit. But I have waited for Thy salvation, O Lord.'

Why are the ungodly generally so jocund? asks Thomas Shepard. Partly, he answers, their want of understanding. They may be very eloquent on scenery, and on travel, and on art, and yet the scales may be on their eyes and the shell on their heads all the time as to anything deeper than the surface of things. Most men, he asserts, remain total strangers to themselves, and to their true spiritual state, all their days. And a little after that, this pungentest of preachers goes on to ask why the truly godly are ofttimes so much more sad and melancholy than other people? And among other deep answers he supplies himself and us with this deep answer,—It is not because they are too godly that they are so sad, but because they are not far more godly. They have grace enough to bring them off from casual and worldly delights, but not enough to enable them to live upon the spiritual and eternal world, and to fetch all their comforts from thence. Grace has for ever spoiled their joy in the creature, but they are not yet grown so spiritual as to live upon God alone, and hence it is that they are found so often hovering in sadness and dissatisfaction between earth and heaven. Thomas Shepard's *Ten Virgins*, and his *Zacchæus*, are perfect mines of the profoundest and most experimental truth. Lord Brodie also will give us his testimony on this same subject out of his heavy-hearted diary. Brodie was not Paul, nor Pascal, nor Bunyan, nor even Thomas Shepard, but he had sufficient heaviness of mind and sorrow of heart to purchase him a right and a title to be listened to on this matter now in hand. 'I never could allow myself,' he says, 'much exuberant joy in any created thing. But I have always exercised myself to hold every such thing soberly and ready to be surrendered up.' And the truly great Halyburton has much the same thing to tell us. 'The strong power of sin that I found still remaining in me, and the disturbances thence arising, made life not desirable ; and a prospect of final and complete riddance by death, made death appear much more eligible.'

But to come back before we close to what we began with, that is to say, the true place of nature in the religious, and especially in the Christian, life. And instead of offering you my own weak words on such a high subject, take this classical passage out of the diary of Thomas Shepard's great pupil in the things of the soul, the greatest man, Dr.

Duncan is inclined to think, since Aristotle. We all know the use that our Lord makes of nature in His preaching. Well, here are some examples of the uses that Jonathan Edwards makes of nature also. 'Immediately after my conversion, God's excellency began to appear to me in everything— in the sun, in the moon, in the stars, in the waters, and in all nature. The Son of God created this world for this very end, to communicate to us through it a certain image of His own excellency, so that when we are delighted with flowery meadows and gentle breezes of wind we may see in all that only the sweet benevolence of Jesus Christ. When we behold the fragrant rose and the snow-white lily, we are to see His love and His purity. Even so the green trees, and the songs of birds, what are they but the emanations of His infinite joy and benignity? The crystal rivers and murmuring streams, what are they but the footsteps of His favour and grace and beauty? When we behold the brightness of the sun, the golden edges of the evening cloud, or the beauteous rainbow spanning the whole heaven, we but behold some adumbration of His glory and His goodness. And, without any doubt, this is the reason that Christ is called the Sun of Righteousness, the Morning Star, the Rose of Sharon, and the Lily of the Valley, the apple-tree among the trees of the wood, a bundle of myrrh, a roe, and a young hart. But we see the most proper image of the beauty of Christ when we see the beauty of the soul of man.' So far the greatest mind since Aristotle.

XVI

PAUL THE AGED

IT is calculated that the Apostle must have been somewhere between fifty-eight and sixty-four when he wrote of himself to Philemon as Paul the aged. Certain difficulties have sometimes been raised over the text. It has sometimes been asked whether Paul would have spoken of himself as such an old man, say, at sixty, or sixty-three. But a thousand things may come in to make a man feel either old or young at that, or at any other age. The kind of life a man has lived; virtuous or vicious, religious or irreligious, idle or industrious, for himself, or for God and his generation, the state of his health, the state of his fortune, his family life, his disappointed or fulfilled hopes in life, and so on. Cicero wrote his *Cato* at sixty-three, and the great orator's design in that famous dialogue was to brace up those men around him whose knees were beginning to tremble, and their hands to hang down about that time of life. And Cicero goes on to fortify first himself and then his readers, with such examples as those of Plato, who died at his desk at eighty-one; and Isocrates, who wrote one of his best books at ninety-four, and who lived another five years on the fame of it; and Gorgias the Leontine, who completed a hundred and seven years, and never to the end loitered in his love of work, but died leaving this testimony on his deathbed, 'I have had no cause for blaming old age,' he said. 'I, myself,' adds Cato, 'supported the Voconian law at sixty-five with an unimpaired voice and powerful lungs.' And, best of all, at the age of seventy, Ennius lived in such a heart as to bear nobly those two burdens, which are by most men deemed the greatest—poverty and old age. Ennius bore those two burdens with what seemed to all men around him the greatest goodwill. On the other hand, in annotating the text Bishop Lightfoot reminds us that Roger Bacon complained of himself at fifty-three as already an old man. And so too Sir Walter Scott lamented of himself at fifty-five as 'a grey old man.' Now it must be admitted that those two Christians do not come out at all well when set beside the brave-hearted heathens. Only, Dr. Samuel Johnson's shout must not be forgotten—Drink water, Sir, and go in for a hundred! And who himself drank water and went in for reading the best and writing the best, till he published his masterpiece after he was threescore and ten. Dante's old age in the Banquet begins at forty-five. But, on the other hand, Tacitus declares that if he had one foot in the grave, it would not matter, he would still be reading and writing the best.

Now, with all his love and loyalty to Paul, and

with all his perfect understanding of everything connected with Paul, for some reason or other, Luke all but completely fails us as Paul's old age approaches. 'And Paul dwelt two whole years in his own hired house in Rome, and received all that came in unto him, preaching the kingdom of God, and teaching those things which concern the Lord Jesus Christ, with all confidence, no man forbidding him.' These are Luke's very last words to us about Paul. I wish I could believe that these beautiful words described Paul's very last days down to the end. But when Luke, for some reason or other, drops into absolute silence, Paul's own Epistles of the Imprisonment come in to supply us with such affecting glimpses into the Apostle's last days as these. 'I, Paul, the prisoner of Jesus Christ. For whom I am an ambassador in bonds. Be not ashamed of me His prisoner. For my bonds are manifest. This also thou knowest that all those that are in Asia be turned away from me. But the Lord have mercy on the house of Onesiphorus, for he oft refreshed me, and was not ashamed of my chain. For I am now ready to be offered up, and the time of my departure is at hand. Demas hath forsaken me, having loved this present world. Only Luke is with me. The cloke that I left at Troas, when thou comest, bring with thee, and the books, but especially the parchments.' With one foot in the grave, like Tacitus, Paul is still reading books and writing parchments. 'At my first answer no man stood by me, but all men forsook me. Do thy diligence to come to me before winter. You see Paul forsaken, lonely, cold and without his cloke, chained to a soldier, and waiting on one of Nero's mad fits for his martyrdom. Well may Paul say, if in this life only we have hope in Christ, we are of all men most miserable. But Paul has such an anchor within the veil that, amid all these sad calamities, old age and all, he is able to send out such Epistles of faith and hope and love as the Ephesians and the Colossians and the Philippians and the Pastorals and Philemon. Comparing the *Odyssey* with the *Iliad*, Longinus says, 'If I speak of old age, it is nevertheless the old age of Homer.'

I really wish I could prevail with you who are no longer young to put aside, as Butler beseeches you, your books and papers of mere amusement, and to read Cicero's *Cato*, and some of the other old age classics, if only to make those fine books to serve for so many foils in a fresh perusal of the Epistles of the Imprisonment. It is our bounden duty to read a Greek or a Roman masterpiece now and then, such as the *Phædo* or the *Cato*, if only to awaken ourselves again to the immensity of the change that came into this world with the Incarnation and the Resurrection of our Lord. What a contrast between philosophy at its very best in Socrates and Cicero, and the Gospel of our salvation unto everlasting life in Paul's old age Epistles! The whole truth and beauty and nobility of such books as the best of Plato and Cicero is all needed the better to bring out the inconceivable contrast between this world at its very best before

Christ, and the new heavens and the new earth that our Lord brought to this world with Him and left in this world behind Him. How such glorious passages as these shine out afresh upon us after we have just laid down the *Cato* and even the *Phœdo*. Such well-known, but so little realised, passages as these: 'Christ shall be magnified in my body, whether it be by life or by death. For to me to live is Christ, and to die is gain. For I am in a strait betwixt two, having a desire to depart, and to be with Christ, which is far better. For our conversation is in heaven; from whence also we look for the Saviour, the Lord Jesus Christ, who shall change our vile body, that it may be fashioned like unto His glorious body, according to the workings whereby He is able even to subdue all things unto Himself. For I am now ready to be offered, and the time of my departure is at hand. I have fought a good fight, I have finished my course, I have kept the faith. Henceforth there is laid up for me a crown of righteousness, which the Lord, the righteous Judge, shall give me at that day; and not to me only, but unto all them also that love His appearing.' What a man was Paul! If he was a man, as one said. Really and truly, my brethren, it would be well worth your putting yourselves to some expense and some trouble in order to read, say, the Consolations of Cato to your old age, and then to turn to Paul's consolations and comforts. Unless, indeed, you already read your Paul with such understanding, and with such imagination, and with such heart, that you do not need the assistance that Plato and Cicero were raised up and preserved to this day to give you.

Well; after repeated readings lately of the Cato, and the Epistles of the Imprisonment, and the Art of Dying Well, and Jeremy Taylor, and suchlike authors for old age, I will now tell you some of the reflections, impressions, and resolutions, that have been left on my own mind. And take first Paul's so touching message to Timothy about his cloke, and his books, and his parchments. For all that comes in most harmoniously after we have just been reading *Cato* about our keeping on reading and writing our best to the end. Lest you might not be able to lay your hands on what Calvin says about Paul's books, I will copy out the passage for you. 'It is evident from this,' says the prince of commentators, 'that the Apostle has not given over study even when he is preparing himself for death. Where are those men then, who think that they have made so great progress that they do not need any more to persevere? Which of you will have the courage to compare yourself with the Apostle? Still more surely does this passage refute the folly of those fools who, despising books, and neglecting all study, boast of their spiritual inspiration.' And if I might be bold enough to add one word after Calvin. I am not now, alas! a neophyte in these matters, and I will therefore take boldness to say this to you. Read the very best books, and only the very best, and ever better and better the older you grow. Be more and more select, and fastidious, and refined, in your books and in your companions, as old age draws on, and death with old age. I wonder just what books they were that Paul missed so much in his imprisoned and apostolic old age at Rome? It might have been the *Apology*. It might have been the *Phædo*. It might have been the *Cato Major*. It could not possibly have been Moses, or David, or Isaiah, or Micah. You may depend upon it, Paul did not forget his Bible when he was packing his trunk at Troas. You are far better off in the matter of books for your old age than Paul was with his Bible and all. Never, then, be out of your Old, and especially, never be out of your New Testament. As Paul says about prayer, read in your New Testament without ceasing. Never lay it down, unless it is to take up another letter of Samuel Rutherford, or another pilgrim's crossing of the river; or, if you have head enough left for it, another great chapter of the *Saint's Rest*. Nothing else. At least, nothing less pertinent and appropriate to your years and to your immediate prospects. Nothing less noble. Nothing less worthy of yourself. Nothing at all but just those true classics of the eternal world over and over again, till your whole soul is in a flame with them, and till your rapture into heaven seizes upon you with one of them in your hand.

You may remember how a great divine as he grew old was wont, for that and for some other reasons, to go back now and then and take a turn up and down in his unregenerate state. As Paul also was wont to do. For as Paul grew older and saintlier, he the oftener would go back upon the sins of his youth. Paul was like William Taylor, who when asked of God what he would choose for a gift in his old age, answered, repentance unto life. And thus it is that if you are well read in Paul's old-age Epistles you will find far more repentance unto life in his last years, than even in his years of immediate conversion and remorse. You meet with an ever deeper bitterness at sin, and at himself, as time goes on with Paul : and, then, a corresponding amazement at God's mercy. And you will do well to be followers of the Apostle, and the Puritan, and the Presbyterian, in this sinner-becoming practice. Go back, then, deliberately and at length, and take many a good look at the hole of the pit you had dug for yourself, and in which you had made your bed in hell. And come up from the mouth of that horrible pit, and up to that Rock on which you now stand, and see if the result will not be the same in you that it was in Paul and in those two most Pauline of preachers and writers ; see if it will not make you hate sin with a more and more perfect hatred, as also to make you long again, and as never before, to be for ever with the Lord.

And, not only read your very best, but pray

your very best also, and that literally without ceasing. Yes, without one atom of exaggeration, or hyperbole, always and without ceasing. If for no other reason than just to make up a little before you die for ever, for your long life, now for ever past, and in which you have found time for everything but prayer, and for every one but God. Or, have you no children or grandchildren to make up to them also for your neglect of their immortal souls? And have you in this matter ever considered God's acknowledged and accepted servant Job? How with him it always was so, that when the days of his children's feastings again came round, he sent and sanctified them, and rose up early in the morning and offered up burnt-offerings according to the number of them all. When do you offer up for your children, early in the morning, or late at night? Different fathers have different habits. Or, when you go back with Paul and take a turn up and down in your un-regenerate state, do you never come upon slain souls who are now under the altar, and who cry continually concerning you—How long, O Lord, holy and true, dost Thou not judge and avenge our blood on them that dwell on the earth! Pray, O unforgiven old man! Pray without ceasing, all the time that is now left you. And who can tell, if God will turn and repent, and turn away from His fierce anger against you, that you perish not.

And every day and every night over your Paul and your Bunyan and your Rutherford and your

Baxter, and suchlike, practise, as they all did, your imagination and your heart upon Jesus Christ. Practise upon Him till He is far more real to you, and far more present with you, than the best of those people are who have lived all your days in the same house with you. Jesus Christ either is, or He is not. If He is not, then there is nothing more to be said. But if He is, then set aside every one else, and practise His presence with you, and your presence with Him. Imagine Christ. Make pictures by that splendid talent that God has given you for the very purpose of making pictures to yourself of Christ. Make pictures to yourself of your meeting with Christ immediately after death. Forefancy your deathbed, said Samuel Rutherford. It was the forefancying of his deathbed that was the conversion and salvation of that old man to whom Rutherford sent the letter. Do you ever forefancy your first meeting with Christ? How do you think He will look? How and where will you look? Rehearse the scene, and have your part ready. It is to the old alone, be it clearly understood, that these things are spoken. The young, and the middle-aged, and those who are busy with other things than preparing to meet with Christ, and with other books than the above—they have plenty of time. But neither you nor I. Let us, at any rate, be up and doing. Santa Teresa felt a thrill go through her every time the clock struck in the church tower. The same thrill, as she had been told, that all our earthly brides feel each time their too slow clock strikes. An hour nearer seeing Him! she exclaimed, and clapped her hands. Up, all you old people, and be like her. Up, and make yourselves ready. Up, and abolish death. Up, out of your bondage all your days through fear of death. Up, and practise dying in the Lord, till you take the prize. Up, and read Paul without ceasing, and pray without ceasing, till you also shall stand on tiptoe with expectation and with full assurance of faith. Yes; up, till you also shall salute His sudden coming, and shall exclaim, Even so, come quickly, Lord Jesus!

FIVE SERMONS ON PAULINE
TEXTS

FIRST SERMON

THE BLOOD OF GOD

THE CHURCH OF GOD, WHICH HE HATH PURCHASED WITH HIS OWN BLOOD.—Acts xx. 28.

THERE is a well-known device in first-class composition whereby a great author gives his readers a sudden stroke of surprise; and that is when he substitutes quite another name for the ordinary and the expected name of the person concerning whom he is writing. All our best literature is full of this ancient rhetorical device; Holy Scripture is full of it, and the text is a case in point. The readers of the Apostle would have expected him to say: The Church of God, which He hath purchased with the blood of His Son; or, with the blood of Jesus Christ; or, with the blood of the Lamb. But by this new and unique way in which the Apostle words this great scripture, he startles his readers into still more wonder and worship than if he had been content to employ one of those far more usual names of our Lord. In this very bold passage the Apostle sets the sin-atoning death of Jesus Christ before us with the veil of His flesh withdrawn, as it were, for a moment. In this almost too bold scripture, he sets before us the pure and immediate Godhead of our Lord made sin for us. And the immense impression that these almost too awful words, the blood of God, make on our minds and our hearts as often as we return to them, is the Apostle's complete justification and rich reward for his almost too bold employment of those awful words.

1. Now, in the first place, what an unspeakable evil sin must be! We would not have been altogether ignorant of the awful evil of sin, even if it had not gone the length of the blood of God. We could not have shut our eyes to the way that sin has cursed and enslaved the soul of man. Death here, and hell hereafter, would surely have burned something of the diabolical evil of sin into the most sin-seared conscience and into the most stone-hardened heart. But all the sick-beds, and all the death-beds, and all the lazar-houses, and all the mad-houses, and all the battle-fields, and all the desolated homes, and all the broken hearts of men and women, from the fall of man to the day of judgment, would not have proclaimed to earth and heaven and hell the unspeakable malice and wickedness of sin. God's own blood, shed by sin, and shed for sin; that alone, in all the universe, is the full measure of the infinite evil of sin. 'Whatever your thoughts about sin may be; whatever your experience and estimate of sin may be, that is My experience and estimate of sin,' says Almighty God, pointing us to Gethsemane and to Calvary. God the Son, made a curse, that

and that alone is the true measure of sin: that and that alone has for ever revealed the true evil of sin: and that and that alone has paid the uttermost farthing for our everlasting redemption and deliverance from sin. 'Let it be counted folly, or phrenzy, or fury, or whatsoever,' says Hooker, in what is perhaps the greatest sermon in the English language; 'it is our wisdom and our comfort. We care for no other knowledge in the world but this, —that man hath sinned and God hath suffered: that God hath made Himself the sin of men, and that men are made the righteousness of God.'

2. And then, what a glorious seal has been set to the holiness of the law of God by His own blood. No wonder that the holy law of God was proclaimed to be magnified, and made honourable for ever, when the very blood of the Lawgiver Himself was shed in order to vindicate and redress the broken law. The throne of God had been founded in righteousness from everlasting. But after a full satisfaction for sin had been made with His own blood who had sat on that throne from everlasting, that glorious throne was for ever established in righteousness as never before. How surpassingly illustrious has the holiness of the law of God shone out on all earth and heaven ever since that day when He whose holy law it was, shed His own blood in atonement to the holiness and the inviolability of that law !

And not His own blood at its last and completed outpouring only. But, along with that, take all the things of the same kind that led up to

His bloodshedding on the tree, and all the things
that entered into that last bloodshedding. Take
all His holy obedience, and all His holy endurance
of all kinds in His body, and in His soul, and in
His spirit, from His circumcision to His crucifixion.
For all that was paid by Him, first in tribute,
and then in atonement, to His own holy law.
And it was all paid for us. Is all our daily and
hourly sin so much bold rebellion against God,
and all done in despite of God's holy law? Then
see, standing over against our rebellion, the complete, and perfect, and most willing subjection and
obedience in everything of God the Son. Are we
by nature, and on every temptation to it, full of
malice towards God and man? Look, over against
that, at our Lord's love to God and man. Look
at His unbounded goodness of heart and life. Is
there bitter repining, and envying, and grudging
in our hearts at the good of our neighbour? Then
let us lift our eyes and look at the Son of God,
how He made Himself of no reputation, and re-
joiced at the prospect of His sharing His glory with
us all for ever. Hear Him, O jealous and grudging hearts! 'I thank thee, O Father, that Thou
hast loved them as Thou hast loved Me.' And so
on through the whole of His life of suretyship
obedience, and on to the end of His death of
atonement, till His own holy law was satisfied
and vindicated to its very utmost height and depth
and length and breadth, even to its very innermost
spirituality, in every thought and word and deed
of God the Son as the son of man.

3. But the sinner's guilty conscience is sometimes, and in some men, far more difficult to satisfy and to silence than even the broken law of God. Long after the broken law of God has been magnified and made honourable, the sinner's evil conscience will still hold out against all that can be said or done to restore its lost peace, and to re-establish its lost confidence in the goodwill of God and man. There is a divinely delegated sovereignty in the human conscience; and there is a corresponding uncompromisingness and inappeasableness in the guilty conscience. Even after the offended sovereign is satisfied, the viceroy still holds out against the disloyalty and the treachery. The *crimen læsæ majestatis*, the high misdemeanour done against the crown, is far more resented and avenged by the king's judges than even by the king himself. And sin is such an unpardonable misdemeanour against all law and all authority, and it so gashes the conscience and so horrifies the heart of the truly penitent sinner, that absolutely nothing has ever been discovered to heal and to quiet and to restore the conscience but the blood of Him who is God. There is no physician for the sinner's exasperated conscience, as Luther is always saying, but the Lord of the conscience Himself. And there is no balm that even He can bring to bear on a thoroughly bad conscience, but His own blood. Your guilty conscience can have nothing better than the blood of your God. And if that does not cleanse, and quiet, and heal your guilty conscience, it must just

rage on. Your conscience can be offered nothing on earth or in heaven beyond the blood of God.

4. One of the ways in which the blood of God comes to have such sovereign virtue in the sinner's conscience is this. When our consciences toward one another are wounded, and are full of remorse and fear, nothing will heal the wound and restore peace between man and man, nothing but a great uprising of love between the alienated parties. But if a great enough uprising and outgoing of love takes place between them, then not only is the lost peace restored, but those who were once such enemies are henceforth far better friends than ever they were before. And the same noble law of reconciling love holds even more in the world of sin and salvation. The blood of God the Son is such a manifestation of divine love toward the sinner that nothing can resist it. No guilt, no remorse, no terror, no suspicion, can stand out against the love of God in the blood of His only begotten Son. It is not so much our Surety's payment of the uttermost farthing of our debt that heals our horrified consciences. It is not His atoning blood even that so pacifies, and so conquers, and gives such peace, to the guilty conscience. It is the love of God as seen in the atonement that can alone do all that. And if there are still any of the dregs of remorse, and terror, and irreconcilability, and suspicion, in your conscience toward God, it is not because His blood is not of volume and virtue enough to wash away all your sins; but it is because you do not open your

heart wide enough and deep enough to receive His love. For there is no fear in love. But perfect love on God's part to you, awakening on your part a corresponding love to God, such perfect love on both sides casteth out all possible fear, so much so, that he that feareth is not made perfect in love.

My brethren, I can recommend this great Scripture to every guilty conscience and corrupt heart. For, times and occasions without number, when every other Scripture has threatened to fail myself, this Scripture has been a rock and a refuge to me. The very awfulness of the word used has again and again silenced the almost as awful accusation of my conscience and the almost as awful despair of my heart. I know all that has been said against the above reading in this glorious passage ; but once read by me I shall never let it go, though I have to hold it against all the world. The BLOOD OF GOD has an inward, and an experimental, and an all-satisfying evidence to me : and I recommend it to you with all my heart.

SECOND SERMON

FAITH IN HIS BLOOD

BEING JUSTIFIED FREELY BY HIS GRACE THROUGH THE REDEMPTION THAT IS IN CHRIST JESUS: WHOM GOD HATH SET FORTH TO BE A PROPITIATION THROUGH FAITH IN HIS BLOOD: FOR THE REMISSION OF SINS THAT ARE PAST, THROUGH THE FORBEARANCE OF GOD: TO HIM WHICH BELIEVETH IN JESUS.—Rom. iii. 24-26.

'THE happy period was now arrived which was to shake off my fetters. I flung myself into a chair near the window, and seeing a Bible there I ventured once more to apply to it for comfort and instruction. The first verse I saw was the 25th of the third of the Romans : " Whom God hath set forth to be a propitiation through faith in His blood." Immediately I received strength to believe, and the full beams of the Sun of Righteousness shone upon me. I saw the sufficiency of the atonement that Christ had made. I saw my pardon sealed in His blood. I saw all the fulness and completeness of His righteousness for me. In a moment I believed and received the atonement.' So writes William Cowper in his Memoirs of his early days.

'Being justified freely by His grace.' The Apostle does not say—being foreknown, or being predestinated, or being adopted, or being sanctified, or being glorified. He will say all these things afterwards; at the proper time and to the proper persons. But not now, and not yet. For the Apostle has before him at this moment an audience of sinful men; an audience of men whose mouths, in the Apostle's own words, are stopped because of their guilt before God. And Paul speaks to that, and confines himself to that. A guilty and a condemned man may need much to be done for him afterwards. But his immediate need; his first need that makes all his other needs to be forgotten, is his need of pardon. Get his pardon sealed, and his prison door set open—that is the one thing needful for him at the present moment. And thus it is that Paul addresses the whole of this great passage to those men whose mouths are stopped, and his great gospel message to all such men is this: their free and full justification before God, and their acceptance and peace with God.

But what is this justification concerning which so much is said by the Apostle? 'Justification is an act of God's free grace, wherein He pardoneth all our sins, and accepteth us as righteous in His sight, only for the righteousness of Christ imputed to us, and received by faith alone.' You cannot have justification better defined than that, unless it is in the Larger Catechism and the Confession of Faith. One of the first death-beds I ever attended in this city had this impressive and memorable fact about it. The dying man had always the Confession of Faith open on his pillow, and open at the chapter on justification. And as his end drew near, he and I often read this rich section together : ' Those whom God effectually calleth, He also freely justifieth ; not for anything wrought in them, or done by them, but for Christ's sake alone ; by imputing the obedience and the satisfaction of Christ unto them, they receiving and resting upon Christ, and upon His righteousness by faith ; which faith they have not of themselves, it is the gift of God.' ' I sink in deep waters,' cried another dying man. ' All His waves and His billows go over me.' Then said the other, ' Be of good cheer, my brother. I feel the bottom, and it is good.'

' Being justified freely by His grace.' This is an instance of what the rhetoricians call reiteration and tautology. Strictly speaking, and speaking coldly, it would be enough to say either ' freely,' or to say—' by His grace.' Both expressions, taken literally and severely, are not needed. But there are some things that cannot be reiterated too often, and free grace is one of them, and is the chiefest of them. You cannot tell me too often, or with too much emphasis, that I am a forgiven sinner, and that not for works of righteousness that I have done, but by the free grace of God. And besides, the style is the man. Paul's style is Paul and Paul alone. Paul is here preaching his own experience, and his own thoughts and feelings about his own experience deeply colour and warmly enrich his style of writing. He is telling here to all that fear God what God in His free grace has done for his soul. Let this great reiteration therefore stand, if only it helps in any degree to encourage and comfort a single sinner, or to assure a single saint. Let it stand, indeed, in letters of gold a finger deep. For it is 'grace dyed in grace,' as Goodwin says. And again, it is 'gracious grace.' Let it stand; for too frequent or too emphatic repetition is impossible in this great matter here in hand.

'For the remission of sins that are past through the forbearance of God.' A great preacher of Paul's gospel, as often as his conscience became untender; as often as his faith and love and holiness threatened to fall asleep; was wont to awaken himself by going back and taking a turn up and down among the sins of his unregenerate state, and that never failed, so he tells us, to bring him to his senses. Now, whether we are regenerate or unregenerate, we should be like that great evangelical preacher. We should, from time to time, and frequently, take a turn up and down among our past sins. It would do us good. It would break our hearts, indeed, but it would be our salvation. Let us therefore, and not seldom, go back upon ourselves and say, 'Look, O my soul, at thy past self, and past through the forbearance of God. Look at that place where thou didst once dwell, and in which thou didst live a life of such sin. And look at that person—where is he now?—thy companion in thy sin. And look often at

those things in thy past that no one ever saw but
God Himself, whose forbearance toward thee and
toward thy sins has been so long and so great.'
And when your heart turns sick as you go back
upon your past, betake yourself again to Cowper's
passage, and to Him whom God hath set forth to
be a propitiation through faith in His blood, for
the remission of sins that are past through the
forbearance of God.

'To declare, I say, at this time His righteousness.' 'This time' to Paul was just that moment
when he sat, pen in hand, over this passage.
And then 'this time' to the Romans was the
first time they read this passage, or again heard
it read. But their time is now long past, and
our time has this day come to us. This, in Paul's
words in another epistle of his, is our accepted
time, and our day of salvation. Now, is it so?
Or is it to be so? All our past sins close round
us at this time, beseeching us to seek their remission before the time of remission is for ever
past. Now what is your answer? What are you
intending to do with those sins that are past, but
are past only through the forbearance of God?
Are you to go on counting on His continued
forbearance? Or will you not make His long-
suffering your salvation, and at this time cast
yourself and all your sins on His free and full
forgiveness? Which of the two is it to be at this
time? It is for you to say. For neither God
nor man can say it for you. Only, as ambassadors
for Christ, as though God did beseech you by us,

we pray you in Christ's stead, be ye reconciled to God, that God may in your case also be just, and the justifier of him which believeth in Jesus.

And then, 'him which believeth in Jesus' will be your true and proper name from this time henceforward. And when once you have attained to that great name, hold fast by it. At all times and in all places look on yourself, and give this always as your true and proper name and address, 'him which believeth in Jesus.' As often as you join that great gospel preacher, and take a turn with him up and down among the sins that are past, always begin that review and end it as a believer in Jesus. Never, for one moment, dare to face either your past sins or your present sinfulness, but as a believer in Jesus. And if you have been a great transgressor in the past, and still are a great sinner in your heart, then, all the more, be a great believer in Jesus. Whatever other parts you may, or may not, play in life : whatever other characters you may, or may not, sustain : whatever other designations or descriptions you may, or may not, answer to,—be in all, and be above all, a believer in Jesus. All your days, and above everything else, practise believing in Jesus till you become an adept in that most important of all the arts and accomplishments of human life in this world. And then when your believing days on earth come to an end,—What benefits do believers receive from Christ at death? The souls of believers are, at their death, made perfect in holiness, and do immediately pass into glory, and their bodies being still united to Christ, do rest in their graves till the resurrection. And then,—What benefits do believers receive from Christ at the resurrection? At the resurrection, believers being raised up in glory, shall be openly acknowledged and acquitted in the day of judgment, and made perfectly blessed in the full enjoying of God to all eternity. Lord, I believe, help Thou mine unbelief!

THIRD SERMON

HIM THAT WORKETH NOT

*TO HIM THAT WORKETH NOT,
BUT BELIEVETH ON HIM THAT
JUSTIFIETH THE UNGODLY,
HIS FAITH IS COUNTED FOR
RIGHTEOUSNESS.*—Rom. iv. 5.

EVERY great science, every great art, every
great doctrine and discipline, has its own
special terminology; its own technical terms, as
we call them. Every new discovery, every new
invention, every new doctrine and development of
doctrine, demands a new name to describe it, to
contain it, and to convey it. Now, though it is
quite true that this word ' work ' is one of our most
familiar words, at the same time, when the Apostle
takes that word up into his great evangelical
vocabulary, he straightway fills that familiar word
of ours full with all the fulness of his own inward
and spiritual meaning. He fills it full with such
new and such deep meanings, that it takes us all
our days to get this one word of his well into our
so inexperienced and so unspiritual minds.

To work, in the ordinary and everyday sense of
that word, is just to do this and that with our
hands. It is to dig, and dress, and keep a garden.

It is to plough, and sow, and reap a field. It is to found, and build, and furnish a house. As the fourth commandment has it: Six days shalt thou labour, and do all thy work. But there is a whole world of work that is not comprehended in the fourth commandment. Master, said one in the Gospel, which is the great commandment of the law? Jesus said to him, Thou shalt love the Lord thy God with all thy heart, and with all thy strength, and with all thy mind, and thy neighbour as thyself. Now that is the commandment, and that is the work, which the Apostle is continually treating of, and not the six days' work of the fourth commandment. The grand commandment of love embraces not only all that we do both Sabbath-day and week-day, but much more all that we think both Sabbath-day and week-day, and all that we feel, and all that we desire, and all that we long after. To work, in the Apostle's employment of the word, is every beat of our heart, and every tone of our voice, and every glance of our eye; it is every sigh of ours and every smile. All we are, and all we have, and all we do, must be wholly given up to God and our neighbour, just as God gives up Himself and our neighbour to us. For God is love, and love is the fulfilling of all God's holy law.

Now, that being so, is it not a very startling thing that the Apostle should say here what he does say? Should say that to him that worketh not: that is to say, to him who loves neither God nor his neighbour aright, such and such great blessings are offered to him, and are indeed pressed upon him? What does the Apostle mean? One thing is certain, he cannot mean what, at first sight, he seems to mean. He cannot mean that the man who does not endeavour with all his might to love and serve both God and his neighbour, can ever stand accepted before God. No. But he has the mind of Christ and the message of God to us when he says authoritatively and conclusively: To him that worketh not: that is to say, to him who cannot work; to him who, as God is his witness, would work if he were only able; to him who agonises day and night to do this work of works, and who has for ever given up agonising after anything else; to him who sets God and his neighbour before him in everything; but the things he would fain do, both to God and his neighbour, he cannot attain to them; with all his sweat, and with all his tears, and with all his prayers, he cannot attain to them so as to come near performing them. He works his fingers to the bone; he bows his back to the burden; but with it all, and after it all, at the end of every day he lays down his day's work toward God and his neighbour, not only not done, but much further from being done than it was when he took it up. Oh, wretched man that he is! who shall deliver him from the body of this death? For we know that whatsoever the law saith, it saith to them that are under the law, that every mouth may be stopped, and all the world may become guilty before God.

But what is this that is here preached from God to every man whose mouth is so stopped? What is this new thing 'believing,' to which such great blessings are everywhere promised? Well, the very first step of all believing to everlasting life is to believe what is written in the New Testament concerning Jesus Christ. At the same time, I may believe every word that Matthew and Mark and Luke and John ever write about Jesus of Nazareth, just as I believe what Plutarch and Tacitus write about Julius Cæsar, and yet be no better. That is to say, I may believe my New Testament with what our divines are wont to call an historic faith. Nay, I might even have actually stood on Calvary, and might have seen with my own eyes Jesus Christ on the Cross, and all the time not gone down to my house justified. To be justified by faith I must go on to believe that God hath set forth His Son to be a propitiation for sin, through faith in His blood, and I must place all my faith in His blood, as if He had come and had died on the Cross for me alone. As Walter Marshall has it : ' The former of these acts of believing doth not immediately unite us to Christ, because it termineth only on the gospel. Yet it is a saving act, so far as it goes, because it instructeth and inclineth and dis-poseth the soul to the latter act, whereby Christ Himself is immediately received into the heart. He that believeth the New Testament with hearty love and liking, as the most excellent truth, will certainly, with the like heartiness, believe on Christ for his salvation.' And thus, true saving faith, once rooted in any man's heart, will, under the hand of the Holy Ghost, grow up to the full assurance of faith, as we see it in such great examples of full assurance as Abraham, the father of the faithful in the Old Testament, and Paul himself, the great preacher and pattern of faith in the New Testament.

But though Walter Marshall is preaching Paul's gospel when he makes the saving act of faith to terminate on Christ and in His blood, at the same time, in this text, as so often in other texts, the Apostle carries up our faith beyond even Christ, and beyond even His blood, and rests our faith ultimately and finally on God the Father. In the Apostle's soteriology our salvation takes its first rise in the love and the grace of the Father, and then both the Son and the Spirit perform each their proper part in carrying out the Father's will. And thus it is that in this great text Paul runs our faith up to God the Father Himself, and instructs us to make our approach to Him alone as the ' justifier of the ungodly.' But we greatly stagger at that name of God, as at so many other of His names. When we first hear this immoral doctrine, the justification of the ungodly, we will not have it. In the interests of truth and righteousness, and for the honour of God, we will not listen to it. That the ungodly should be justified, and the ungodly alone—far be it from us to believe such antinomian teaching! We can understand the godly being justified, or even the partly godly and the partly un-

godly; but not the utterly ungodly. But so
it is. In the gospel this is one of the many
mysteries of godliness, that God justifieth the
ungodly, and the ungodly alone; and that as
ungodly, and always as ungodly. The more
ungodly indeed any man is, the more fit and
eligible he is for justification. It was the godliness of the Pharisee that was his ruin. And it
was the utter absence of all godliness in the
publican that made it possible to send him to his
house justified. And so is it in this temple to-day
also. Show me the man among you who feels
himself to be the most ungodly man in the whole
congregation. Show me the man who feels himself to be absolutely made of sin, like David and
Paul, and I will show you the man who is the
ripest of you all for his free and full justification;
and who, if he will only add to his utter ungodli-
ness the faith of the text, will go down to his
house established in that peace of conscience
which passes all understanding.

This doctrine of justification by faith is like
one of the doctrines of the old manuscripts. The
more difficult to receive any offered reading of an
old manuscript, the more unlikely to be true,
the harder the lection, the more the scholars trust
it, and take it, and incorporate it. Now there is
nothing offered to us in the whole region of salvation so hard to receive, and believe, and hold by,
as just the doctrine of the text. The Jews would
not have it; they stoned Paul because he preached
it. The whole apostleship itself was up in arms

against him because of it. They condemned it as an antinomian doctrine, and they denounced him who preached it. But it held the field, and it will more and more hold the field wherever it is preached in faith, and prayer, and alongside of a holy life, as Paul preached it, and as Luther, and Hooker, and Bunyan, and Marshall, and all the Puritans, and Chalmers, and all his sons, preached it in Scotland. 'I should be glad to know,' wrote Luther to Spentein, an Augustinian monk, 'what is the state of your soul. When you and I were living together we were both in the greatest of all errors: seeking to stand before God on the ground of our own works. I am still struggling against that fatal error, and have not even yet entirely triumphed over it. O, my dear brother, learn to know Jesus Christ, and Him crucified. Beware of pretending to such purity as no longer to confess thyself the chief of sinners. If our labours, and obediences, and afflictions, could have given peace to the conscience, why should Christ have died on the cross? You will never find true peace till you find it and keep it in this: that Christ takes all your sins upon Himself, and bestows all His righteousness on you.' And when the Reformation had brought back the pulpit of England to the Epistle to the Romans, and to the article of a standing or falling Church, Richard Hooker preached thus in his immortal sermon on Justification. I feel as if I could never re-peat the passage too often,—'Christ hath merited righteousness for as many as are found in Him.

And in Him God findeth us if we be believers. For by believing we are incorporated into Christ. Then, although in ourselves we be altogether sinful and unrighteous, yet even the man who is in himself impious, full of iniquity, full of sin; him being found in Christ through faith, and having his sins in hatred through repentance— him God beholdeth with a gracious eye, and accepteth him in Jesus Christ, as perfectly righteous as if he had fulfilled all that is commanded in the holy law of God—shall I say accepteth him as more perfectly righteous than if himself had fulfilled the whole law? I must take heed what I say; but the Apostle saith, "God hath made Him to be sin for us, who knew no sin; that we might be made the righteousness of God in Him!" Let it be counted folly, or phrenzy, or fury, or whatsoever; it is our wisdom and our comfort. We care for no knowledge in the world but this: that man hath sinned and God hath suffered: that God hath made Himself the sin of men, and that men are made the righteousness of God.'

FOURTH SERMON

UNDER GRACE

YE ARE NOT UNDER THE LAW, BUT UNDER GRACE.—
Rom. vi. 14.

'COMFORT ye, comfort ye my people, saith your God; speak ye comfortably to Jerusalem.' Now, the Apostle Paul comforted the people of God, as they had never been comforted before. So completely did the Apostle fulfil this command, that there arose a sect of Christians in the early Church who held that Paul could be none other than the promised Comforter Himself. Paul in every epistle of his, and especially in his Epistle to the Romans, had so comforted their hearts that those early heretics began to hold that the Apostle must surely be the Holy Ghost Himself made flesh, and ministering among sinful men. 'And I almost agree with them,' said Origen, in his extraordinary admiration of the Apostle Paul. 'That man Paul,' said another, 'if he was a man, and no more.'

Now, in order to get at the full comfort of this great scripture, let us ask, What, exactly, is the law? And what, exactly, is grace? And then we shall the better see what it is to be under the law, and what it is to be under grace.

Well: the law is the law. And the law can never be anything else but just the law. God Almighty is a righteous God. God is righteousness itself. God never can be unrighteous in anything He is, or in anything He says, or in anything He does. God is just even in justifying the ungodly. God is perfect and unspotted righteousness, and the law of God is just His perfect and unspotted righteousness righteously administered over angels and men. When it seemed good to Him, Almighty God in His love and power and wisdom, created in knowledge and righteousness and holiness the race of creatures to which we belong. As Paul has it, mankind was made under the law. And as every law, to be a law, must have its own sanctions and securities, its own rewards and punishments, so had that law under which God made man. 'Of every tree of the garden thou mayest freely eat ; but of the tree of the knowledge of good and evil thou shalt not eat of it : for in the day thou eatest thereof thou shalt surely die.' A law of God, with a sanction and a security, a reward and a punishment, alto-gether worthy of such a Lawgiver, and of such law-abiding subjects as Adam and Eve had it in their power and their free will to be : they, and their children. And from that primeval law there were drawn out afterwards the ten command-ments of the Old Testament, and the two commandments of the New Testament : perfect love to God, and perfect love to all men. Now, we know that whatsoever the law saith, it saith to them who are under the law, that every mouth may be stopped, and all the world may become guilty before God. That is the law, and that is what it is to be under the law.

And then, what is grace? Grace is love. But grace is not love simply, and purely, and alone. Grace and love are, in their innermost essence, one and the same thing. Only, grace is love adapting itself to certain special circumstances. As, for instance, love may exist between equals, or it may rise to those who are above it, or it may flow down to those who are beneath it. But grace has only one direction that it can take. Grace always flows down. And thus it is that sovereigns are said to be gracious to their subjects. But though a subject may loyally and truly and devotedly love his sovereign, yet the most loving of subjects is never said to be gracious to his sovereign. Because grace always flows down. Now, among many other relations that God holds to us, He is our Sovereign, and therefore His love to us is always called His sovereign grace. It is called mercy also, because we are in misery on account of our sin. But it is called grace above all, because we are not only in an estate of sin and misery, but because we are so infinitely beneath God, and are in that and in every other way so utterly unworthy of His love. And thus it is that with its infinite condescension toward us, grace has the most absolute freeness in all its outgoings and down-flowings also. And as grace is free, so is it sure. Nothing can change, or alter, or turn away, sovereign grace. And, with all that, it is unconditional. That is to say, as no merit of mortal man ever drew down on him the grace of God, so no demerit and no ill-desert of any man on whom it has once rested, will ever cause that grace to be withdrawn. It is not of works, lest any man should boast. Therefore it is of faith, that it might be by grace; to the end the promise might be sure to all the seed. If by grace, then it is no more of works; otherwise grace is no more grace. Grace, then, is grace,—that is to say, it is sovereign, it is free, it is sure, it is unconditional, and it is everlasting.

Now from all this, keep it always well in mind, that the law is the law, and that grace is grace. And that the law can never say but this one thing: Do and live. And every day that you try to do the law of God, and to live by doing it, you will be right glad to remember that the law is the law, and that grace is grace. For if the law continually commands what you cannot do, then and there grace comes forward, always true to herself: always promising, and offering, and bestowing. 'The gospel,' says John Wesley, 'is one great promise.' Just as the law is one great command. Keep that deep and everlasting distinction and difference ever before you, and continually make application of it to all that is within you. And that simple definition and distinction, kept ever in mind, will save you many a hard day and many a dark night. Keep well under grace, as the text has it. Be well taught in grace. Read the books of grace. Sit under the preachers of grace. Offer the prayers of grace. Sing the psalms, and hymns, and spiritual songs, of grace. And do the works of grace. For grace has her own works also. Then said they unto Him, What shall we do that we might work the works of God? Jesus answered, and said unto them : This is the work of God, that ye believe on Him whom God hath sent. And again, this is His commandment, that we should believe on the name of His Son Jesus Christ, and love one another, as He gave us commandment. Learn to say about grace what Paul said on Mars' hill about the God both of nature and of grace. Learn to say, For in grace we live, and move, and have our being. You cannot say that about the law. Paul, with all his obedience, could not say that about the law. ' I was alive without the law once,' says Paul about himself ; ' but when the commandment came, sin revived, and I died.' For the law always kills. It came, indeed, to kill, in order that grace might make alive. If life could have come by the law, then grace had come in vain. No mortal man has ever lived, to be called life, under the law. But grace brings true and everlasting life. Live, then, in grace, and in nothing else. Rise up every morning in grace. Congratulate yourself every morning as you awake, and say, O my soul, we are not under the law, but under grace. Go out to your day's work under grace. And return home, and lie down on your bed again, ever more and more under grace. Live, and die, and rise again, and go to judgment, and go to heaven itself, and all under grace. The last words of Mr. Honest were, Grace reigns. So he left the world.

FIFTH SERMON

THE LIFE OF FAITH

THE JUST SHALL LIVE BY FAITH.—Rom. i. 17.

THE Bible, both Old Testament and New, is full of faith and the life of faith. The Bible may be said to be a book for believers and for believers alone. You need not open the Bible unless you are already a believer, or are willing, by its help, to become a believer. For, from Genesis to Revelation, the Bible is written by believers, about believers, and for believers. The Hebrew prophets preached all their sermons to believers, and the Hebrew psalmists composed all their psalms for the use of believers. And, coming down to New Testament times, Jesus Christ Himself began His life on earth by being nothing else but a believer. All His life on earth he went about looking everywhere for believers. And as often as He found another believer, that gave Him meat to eat that other men knew not of. And open Paul where you please, and you have faith and the life of faith in every epistle of his. If any epistle has not faith and the life of faith in it, you may be sure it is no true epistle of the Apostle Paul. Paul himself, after the Man Jesus Christ, was the greatest believer that ever lived. And he will make you the greatest believer now living, if you will give your days and nights to nothing else but to his epistles. And, if you are well advised, you will do that. For there is no other occupation of the mind for one moment to be compared with the study of Paul on the objects of faith and on the life of faith. It is the most intellectual of all studies, and it is the most spiritual of all studies, and it is the only study that you will take up again in heaven just at the point where you laid it down at the moment of your death on earth. Faith, in all her objects, and in all her exercises, is the very queen of studies. All other arts and sciences, all other literatures and philosophies, all other pursuits and accomplishments are, at their very best, but the companions and the handmaidens of faith.

And then, faith is such a sovereign that she has a whole universe of things under her sole and sovereign sway. As the whole world of things tangible is wholly put under our sense of touch ; and as the whole world of things visible is wholly given up to our sense of sight ; and as that other world of things audible belongs to our sense of hearing, and to that sense alone : so is the whole unseen world, and all that it contains, absolutely delivered over to our faith. So much is this the case, that the whole spiritual and eternal world has as good as no existence to him who has not faith. In the words of inspiration—they have no substance and no evidence to him who has not faith. Almighty God, His Son Jesus Christ, the atoning blood and the justifying righteousness of Jesus Christ; heaven and its everlasting blessedness; and all the things that are akin to these things, have no existence to him who has not faith. And no man needs Holy Scripture to tell him that. We all know that in ourselves. There are times with us all when to us there is neither God nor Christ, nor heaven nor hell. And again, there are other times when there is nothing in all the world but just these unseen things. All these things come and go to us just according to our faith. Nothing could be a better definition and description of faith than just that famous definition and description, that faith is the substance of things hoped for, the evidence of things not seen.

Now, the just shall live by faith, says the Apostle in the text. Yes. But who, exactly, are the just, and where are they to be found among sinful men? My brethren, the only just man is the man who has been justified. He is the same man whose mouth was once stopped and which has never again been opened to justify himself, and who has therefore been taken by God and has been justified and accepted in His Son Jesus Christ. But what exactly is it to be justified? What is justification? *Justification is an act of God's free grace, wherein He pardoneth all our sins, and accepteth us as righteous in His sight, only for the righteousness of Christ imputed to us and received by faith alone.* That, then, is the just man of the text. There is no other just man, nor will ever be. The only just man is the justified man of the Epistle to the Romans and the Shorter Catechism. And he will know, and will be sure, that he is a justified man just according as he lives by faith.

And he lives, for one thing, by his faith in his Bible. The Bible is more to every believer than his necessary food. O how love I Thy law! is his constant ejaculation. It is my meditation all the day. More to be desired are they than gold, yea, than much fine gold. Sweeter also than honey and the honeycomb. The Psalms are written in letters of gold to the eye of faith, and the Epistle to the Romans is the very marrow of lions to the taste of faith. Show me a believing man, and I will show you a justified man, and, withal, a man who is never out of his Bible. What else would you have him to read? I would like to hear you urging some of your favourite reading on him. I would like you to tell him where else but in his Bible such faith as his could be fed. Where else could he get songs for the house of his pilgrimage? And shoes for his feet, and a staff for his hand? And his whole furniture for his life of faith, and for his death of victory? Yes: depend upon it, the just man will live, and move, and have his whole being, in his Bible, and in books that have been drawn out of his Bible.

But the just man's Bible is all that to him,

because Christ is in his Bible. To me to live is Christ, is Paul's constant protestation. Christ is everything to Paul: absolutely everything. Christ is made of God to Paul wisdom, and righteousness, and sanctification, and redemption. Name anything to Paul that you think he needs; claim anything from Paul that you think he owes you; put Paul into any position you like, even into prison, even into death and hell itself, and Paul is, that moment, complete in Christ. But, while all fulness dwells in Christ, it is His blood that Paul's faith is found dealing with oftenest. Never had any man's faith a bolder scope, or a vaster sweep, than Paul's faith in Christ. But it is on Christ's blood that Paul's faith oftenest gazes, and always puts its trust. 'The object of faith,' says Dr. Christian Baur in his great book on Paul, 'is narrowed in Paul stage by stage. And in proportion as this is done, Paul's faith becomes more intense and more inward. From mere theoretical assent Paul's faith becomes a practical trust, which has for its one object the blood of Christ.' Exactly true, and excellently said. There is no limit to the scope and sweep of Paul's faith. Everything that Christ is as the God-Man; everything that Christ has done, is doing, or ever will do, is all Paul's by faith. But, here and now, it is His blood that is the one thing needful to Paul, and compared with which, there is nothing else for one moment to be called needful. Paul preached Christ in all His offices as He has never been preached since. But all the time Paul was such a

sinner, and he was preaching to such sinners, that
Christ crucified was his one determination as a
preacher. They are his own words: 'For I am determined not to know anything among you save Jesus
Christ, and Him crucified.' Paul not only at the
gate of Damascus, but even in the apostolic pulpit,
was always in himself a condemned man. But who
is this that cometh from Edom, with dyed garments
from Bozrah? Wherefore art thou red in thine
apparel, and thy garments like him that treadeth
the winefat? Lo! this is He whom God hath
set forth to be a propitiation through faith in His
blood. This is He on whom the LORD laid the
iniquity of us all. Yes: every day, and in every
place, Paul's past sins, and his ever-present sinfulness, would be a millstone about his neck; he
would be beside himself; he would be in hell
already, but for the blood of Christ. Most true,
the just man lives by his faith in his Bible. But
that is so because his Bible is so full to him of the
blood of Christ.

Be believers, then, my brethren. Practise believing continually, and in connection with everything that happens to you. If you have been
great transgressors in the past, and if you are still
great sinners in your heart, be correspondingly
great believers in Christ. Be much in the
believer's Bible, and be less and less in every other
book that does not draw its inspiration out of the
believer's Bible. But, especially, let your faith in
the blood of Christ prosper and grow stronger
and stronger every day. Go about through life

believing in the blood of Christ at all times and in all places. As your sinfulness pours out of your heart upon you continually, never stopping, but running the more the more you try to stop it; so there is over against your sinful heart a fountain filled with blood, and that fountain will flow as long as your sinful heart flows. Have faith in that blood, then. Live by faith in that blood. And when you come to die, die believing in that blood. And, so dying, you will rise again believing for the last time. For at their deaths the souls of believers are made perfect in holiness, and do immediately pass into glory. And then, at the resurrection, believers, being raised up in glory, shall be openly acknowledged and acquitted in the day of judgment, and made perfectly blessed in the full enjoying of God to all eternity. Amen.

AN APPRECIATION

OF

WALTER MARSHALL

THE MOST PAULINE OF DIVINES

WALTER MARSHALL

AND HIS BOOK, 'THE GOSPEL-MYSTERY OF SANCTIFICATION

AN APPRECIATION

WILLIAM COWPER writes thus in one of his classical letters : 'The book you mention lies now on my table. Marshall is an old acquaintance of mine. I think Marshall one of the best writers, and one of the most spiritual expositors of Scripture I ever read. I never met a man who understood the plan of salvation better, or who was more happy in explaining it to others.' And James Hervey, the well-known author of *Theron and Aspasio*, says of Marshall's book : 'It has been one of the most useful books to my own soul. I scarce ever fail to receive spiritual consolation and strength from the perusal of it. And, was I to be banished into some desolate island, possessed of only two books beside my Bible, this should be one of the two, perhaps the very first I would choose.' The saintly Robert Trail also says : 'Mr. Marshall was a holy and retired man, known only to the world by this one book, which is deep, practical, well-connected, and requiring a more than ordinary attention to read it with profit. Its great excellence is that it leads the serious reader directly and immediately to Jesus Christ.' And Adam Gib of Edinburgh used to say of Marshall: ' I have scarcely ever been acquainted with any practical treatise of human product so evangelical, in a thread more correct and a method more exact than this.' ' Did I ever speak to you about Marshall on Sanctification?' asks Dr. Chalmers. 'He is at present my daily companion.' And Dr. Andrew Murray of South Africa says in his introduction to a most excellent abridgment of Marshall: 'There is but one book in the English language admitted by all to be the standard book on sanctification. It is the work of the Rev. Walter Marshall, published in 1692. It has at all times received the highest praise from men of eminence both as theologians and saints.' And Dr. Elder Cumming once said to the present writer: ' Ah! Walter Marshall is just Keswick for theologians and men of mind.' And Dr. Laidlaw in a like conversation : ' Marshall is simply the last word on the subject.'

Walter Marshall's one book is but a small book in bulk, and his life is like his book. He was born in 1638. He was educated at Oxford. He was settled in Hursley. He declared for Presbytery. He was cast out of his parish. He profited greatly himself by his preaching : from its efficacy on his own heart he attained to very uncommon degrees of faith and holiness and comfort. He had been for long in great darkness as to the way of attaining to true holiness and true peace. He consulted Richard Baxter and Thomas Goodwin, among others. After he had confessed to Goodwin many sins in his heart and in his life, Goodwin replied, 'You have forgotten to mention the greatest sin of all. The great sin of not believing on the Lord Jesus Christ both for the remission of sins, and for holiness of heart.'

In reading such authors as Hooker, and Leighton, and Owen, and Goodwin, and Rutherford, and Edwards, we continually come upon this expression,—the mystical union. Now, that is a theological and an experimental expression. The thing is in the Scriptures, though not the exact words. The Scriptures, indeed, are full of the thing. And that so expressive phrase has been coined by our great evangelical theologians in order to convey to the mind a certain picture of that glorious relationship which is constituted between Christ and the soul, when the soul is once truly united to Christ, and is, as it were, incorporated into Christ. Now, Paul is the great apostle of the mystical union. The mystical union is in every epistle of his, it might almost be said that the mystical union is in every chapter of his. For Christ, and the believer in Christ, is Paul's constant theme. We are chosen in Christ before the foundation of the world. We are accepted in the Beloved. It hath pleased the Father that in Him should all fulness dwell. And ye are complete in Him, for in Him dwelleth all the fulness of the

Godhead bodily. Rooted and built up in Him,
we are to grow up into Him in all things, which
is the Head, even Christ. Compared with Christ
and the mystical union of believers with Christ,
Paul as good as knows nothing, either in his
preaching or in his epistles. And in this Marshall
is a 'right Pauline divine,' as Luther says. This
is what Dr. Murray says on this subject. 'In
chapter three Marshall teaches us how in Jesus
Christ a new nature was prepared for the believer ;
how the needed endowments for living holily are
provided for in that new nature, and how this is
communicated to us through our living union with
Christ. The beauty of Marshall's book is that he
makes the Mystical Union the starting-point in
the Christian course. He points out how by faith
the sinner receives Christ and His salvation :
how justification and sanctification are both given
in Christ, and received only through the faith that
unites to Him. In our union to Christ, realised
by faith from day to day, and in each duty we
perform, is the only, but the sufficient, strength for
a holy life.' And Dr. Murray adds, 'Let me in
conclusion urge every believer who longs to understand better the secret of a holy life, to take time
for the study of this little book. He need be
afraid of no new doctrine, though the distinct-
ness and the point may make it appear new. But
let no one imagine that a hasty reading of this
book will do him any good. Let him return and
read more than once or twice, till mind and heart
become familiarised with the blessed truth of a

sinner on earth living and speaking and acting daily and hourly as a saint, and that in the power of a holiness dwelling in heaven, because the life of Jesus is his life. And I cannot but think that such a reader will find our writer to be indeed God's messenger to guide him into God's highway of holiness, and into a life of peace and power before unknown.' Walter Marshall has found an editor worthy of himself in Andrew Murray.

And now, to close with, take one or two of Marshall's many striking sentences that arrest us in the course of our reading of 'The Gospel-Mystery.'

On the law of love he says incidentally,—'Take notice, that the law which is your mark, is exceeding broad, and yet not the more easy to be hit : because you must aim to hit it in every duty of it, with a performance of equal breadth, or else you do not hit it all.' And his whole argument revolves round such a passage as this : 'Many men, who are seriously devout, take a great deal of pains to mortify their corrupted nature by pressing vehemently upon their hearts many motives to holiness; labouring importunately to squeeze good affections out of their hearts, as oil out of a flint. On this account they think the entrance into a holy life to be harsh and unpleasing, because it costs so much struggling with their evil hearts to new-frame them. If they only knew that this way of entrance into a holy life is not only harsh and unpleasant, but altogether impossible; and that the true way to mortify sin and quicken their hearts to holiness is by receiving a new nature out of the fulness of Christ; and that we do no more to the production of a new nature than to the production of original sin, though we do more to the reception of it,—if they only knew this, they might save themselves many a bitter agony, and employ their endeavours to enter in at the strait gate in such a way as would be far more pleasant and successful.' And again : 'The old man, the body of sin, is destroyed in us, not by any wounds that we ourselves can give to it, but by our partaking of that freedom from it, that death unto it, that is already wrought out for us by the death of Christ. Therefore we must be content to leave the natural man vile and wicked, as we found it, until it be utterly destroyed by death, though we must not allow its wickedness.' And again : 'Nature remains wicked, and only wicked, even after we have put on Christ.' And again : 'As our natural corruption was produced originally in the first Adam, and was propagated from him to us: so our new nature is produced first in Christ, and is derived from Him to us; or, as it were, propagated.' And to wind up: 'Christ would have us believe on Him that justifieth the ungodly; and therefore He doth not require us to be godly before we believe. He came as a physician to the sick, and He does not expect that they shall recover their health in the least degree before they come to Him. The vilest sinners are fitly prepared and qualified for this design, which is to show forth the exceeding riches of grace. For this end the law of Moses entered, that the offence might abound : so that, where sin abounded, grace might much more abound.'